SEX BYTES

The Fxcked-Up Truth About Tech & Sex

BY
TechChick

Content Warning

Hey, Clever Human!

This book is rated "One Gigabyte Over 18." (That means grown-ups only.)

Sex Bytes is all about real talk. Expect unfiltered geekery, bold bytes of sexual wisdom, and uncensored conversations about bodies, and all things pleasure, and all things sex-positive.

If frank, sex-positive musings make you clutch your charging cable in horror, or if you're not of legal age where you live, now's your chance to hit "exit" before this gets spicy.

Reader discretion (and curiosity) strongly advised. See you on the wild side!

Contents

Intro

... what a shitshow

The internet didn't ruin sex. We did that all by ourselves. The internet just filmed it. — TechChick

Sex, for a lot of people, is basically a three-step *mission* (and I do mean *mission*): foreplay, fucking, and orgasm. Rinse, repeat.

Too many women only get the middle of the mission; they get fucked over on the first and last.

No wonder half of us end up staring at the ceiling, wondering if anyone's ever going to make our toes curl or just keep drilling for oil, like an oil driller with a busted gauge... just poking around and hoping to strike something wet.

No surprise there's an entire industry trying to fix that soul-sucking, lifeless routine. It's like we can't figure it out on our own without expert help. Left to our own devices, we'd treat sex like assembling

1

IKEA furniture: follow vague steps, ignore the missing parts, and pretend it was supposed to look just like that. Welcome to a lifetime of broken furniture and screwing hell.

Enter the books. The columnists. The certified "sexperts" with laminated credentials and disappointing orgasms. We know for damn sure most of them are full of shit (probably having less sex than we are and doing it worse), but we still read, still watch, still listen. Trying to get it right.

And because sex (naturally, obviously, motherfucking-absolutely) begins with foreplay, that's where this book starts, too.

... the letter that started it all

From the Inbox:

Dear Almighty TC,
I tried to find my girl's G-spot last night. Christ almighty, it was like navigating a minefield. Needless to say, the whole thing blew up in my face. At one point, I thought I found it and started working it like crazy. After a few minutes, she stopped me and screamed for me to answer what the hell I was trying to do to her. She said I had a weird, determined look on my face that made me look like a madman. She actually said I looked "dangerous!" My God, I cannot believe this happened to me when all I wanted was to find that fucking G-spot and make her feel good. I suppose you have some smartass advice that makes me feel even more like an idiot.
I can hardly wait,
Dangerous Bob

Dear Dangerous,

I have a saying that goes, "the pussy is for you, the clit is for her, and the G-spot is, eh, who needs it?" If it makes you feel any better, I think most of the world population wants to know what it is, where the hell it's at, and what the fuck to do with it.

Honestly, the search for the G-spot has left more bedrooms looking like a scene of sexual carnage than a place of pleasure. Sheets twisted, egos bruised, partners wondering if they need a map or a mop. Next time, Bob, maybe ask what feels good before you go diving. Nobody ever found the G-spot by holding their breath and hoping for the best.

— Almighty TC

Heads up: my full rant lives in the *Eating Pussy & Clitoral Confusion* chapter. You'll get there. So buckle up, pervs. Let's get this shitshow started.

... TechChick, the book & the mess

Even now, after reading letters like Bob's, I still can't believe I started answering this stuff.

I've been in sales my whole life. I used to sell things like air freight and communication systems in the real world. Now I sell smut in the virtual one. Turns out, selling orgasms is way easier than selling air freight. At least with smut, everyone's breathing heavy for the right reasons.

One of my early web hustles was running an adult site called *tech-chick.com*. I was the owner and webmaster, or webmistress, technically, since I'm a girl and that's what we called ourselves. That letter from Bob? Just one of thousands that landed in my inbox.

After launching that first adult link site, strangers started emailing with every type of sex question imaginable—some bizarre, some hilarious, and many unexpectedly tender. I had no idea why anyone thought I was qualified to answer anything. I didn't feel qualified to give advice. I barely felt qualified to get my ass out of bed before my morning orgasm.

But people kept asking, so I kept answering. That experiment became Needed Sex Tips, the site's most popular section, and eventually snowballed into this book.

I wrote this book with the straight guy in mind, because that's who was blowing up my inbox. But honestly, if you're here for the filth, the laughs, or the real talk (no matter your flavor), you're in the right place. Welcome to the party.

What you'll find here is a mash-up of reader letters, my responses, true stories, rants, how-to's, and sex-soaked observations from the trenches of porn webmistressing. I don't have a degree in sexology, fuckology, or any other ology. I'm just a woman who ran a bunch of adult sites and learned a hell of a lot through reader emails (and arguably more than any "expert" with a dipshit diploma on their dipshit wall).

Ask any good teacher where they learned the most, and they'll tell you: "My students."

If words like "pussy," "cock," and "clit" (just scratching the surface) offend you, this probably isn't the book for you, which begs the question, why the hell did you buy this book?

Still with me? Good. If you're the type to flinch at the word "moist," you might want to back away now. The rest of us are about to get gloriously filthy. — *TC*

P.S. I think we should all just have more sex and quit talking about it so damn much.

This isn't a sanitized, jargon-wrapped, peer-reviewed tour of human intimacy. Oh Christ, no.

It's messy, raw, often ridiculous, and built from the weirdest, wildest, most sincere questions the sex-curious internet underbelly ever coughed up.

... why a re-release?

Because the questions haven't stopped. If anything, they've gotten louder, more confused, more absurd, and frankly, more important.

Welcome to The Original Sex Bytes.

Not a manual. Not exactly a memoir.

Just a holy-what-the-fuckshit ride.

When the book was first published in 2003, you'd think I'd invented a new way to disappoint people. The haters came out swinging:

—"Disgrace."
—"Corrupting the internet."
—"This has to be a man pretending to be a woman."

(Apparently, only men are allowed to talk about sex with this much honesty.)

My inbox filled up with everything from death threats to marriage proposals. Sometimes from the same person. I'm not motherfucking kidding.

The so-called "sexperts" rolled their bulging conservative eyes. The moral police clutched their fake-ass pearls. And a few brave souls actually thanked me for saying what everyone else was thinking.

But here's the thing: the more they screamed, the more readers wrote in. Turns out, people love a good shitshow, especially when it's about something as universal and messy as sex.

And while the critics were calling for my head and trying to moralize me off the internet, the rest of the world kept reading, laughing, and passing it around like contraband. I got called every name in the book. I also got letters from people who said this was the first time they'd ever read anything about sex that felt this real, without shame or bullshit. That made the beating worth it.

So, I took hits. But I also got a hell of a lot of love too.

And if that's not the internet in a nutshell, I don't know what the fuck is.

Foreplay for Fuck's Sake

... perfect foreplay plotting

Perfect foreplay makes average dick feel like a religious experience. — TechChick

Let's get this straight: foreplay is as crucial as eating pussy properly. Nail those two, and you can fuck up damn near all the rest, and she'll still text you at 3am.

Foreplay isn't optional. It's not "extra credit." It's the goddamn main event before the main event, and half the time, it is the main event. Skip it and you're just another limp, forgettable half-session destined for "I'd rather have sex with my magic wand than this selfish prick again."

Here's where most guys crash and burn: The Plan.
That sad, follow-the-script bullshit:
Squeeze her nipple (just so).
Lick her ear (right after the nipple).
Do her third favorite thing from three weeks ago.
Go down on her for four regulation minutes.
Get her off by the six-minute mark so you can finally stick it in.
Yeah. That plan? Torch it. Salt the earth. Let the ashes fuel the hellfire of your ass-fuck of a routine.

The #1 rule of foreplay? Forget the fucking plan.

Instead, tune in. Watch how she breathes, how she arches, and what makes her shiver. Every gasp is a green light. Every squirm is a signpost. Follow those, not the same old tired playbook.

Start by forgetting your own damn orgasm for once. Stop racing. It's not a sprint to some imaginary finish line. If you're watching the clock, you're not watching her. And trust me, she knows.

It's a long, delicious derailment into a slippery, chaotic mindfuck. Stop trying to do it right. Get wickedly into it. Get into her. Let it be filthy. Let it be fun. Let it be fucking curious again.

Don't touch her like you're checking boxes; touch her like you're getting away with something. Trace her skin like you're reading a secret code in braille, slow, deliberate, desperate to crack what no one else ever has.

Don't kiss her to get somewhere; kiss her like kissing is the end. Don't wait for her to moan. Turn up the heat until she can't help herself. Then take control. Whisper filth in her ear. Then say it nastier. Grab, tease, nibble, sprawl. Get spit on her neck. Get sweat in your hair. Confuse the dog. Make the cat run.

If you're not at risk of waking the neighbors or accidentally dialing 911 with your ass, you're doing it half-assed.

If she squirms? Double down. If she moans, bucks, or grabs the sheets, follow that like your life depends on it. If she says, "Don't stop." Don't you fucking stop.

Let it be raw. Let it be sticky, tangled, and dripping. A messy mess.

When you stop treating foreplay like a means to an end, you become the thing she wants before the sex even starts.

Once you burn the plan, the good shit happens. I've had nights where foreplay was so good, the sex after felt almost unnecessary, like dessert after a five-course feast. And trust me, nobody forgets a meal like that.

That's when the shaking starts. That's when the begging starts. That's when she cums so hard she forgets where she is. That's when you become the bar every poor bastard after you gets measured against.

You want that? You burn the plan. You let go. Blow her fucking mind before you fuck her.

And what do you get in return? You get actual great sex. Not duty sex, not finish-up-you-bastard sex, not "Is she wet enough?" sex. You get an uninhibited, filthy, cock-hungry partner who wants to wreck you. Congrats, you've gone from "who?" to "where have you been all my life?"

All because you finally understood: Foreplay isn't the warm-up. It's the whole ever-loving, motherfucking point. You get everything the plan was supposed to deliver but never could in a million years.

... lip service

Most people write to me about fucking, blowjobs, or whether their dick is big enough to impress a pornstar. But every now and then, I get a romantic. Or maybe just an 18-year-old. Hard to tell.

From the Inbox:

> **Dear TC,**
> Do you have any tips or advice on kissing? I'm not inexperienced or anything, but I'm interested in knowing if there's anything I can do to get more out of it, and for her too. I hope you answer this and I hope it's not lame.
> **Thanks, Mark**

> **Dear TechChick,**
> What are the best secrets you can give on the topic of kissing? Do women like it slow and easy and long, or do they like it fast and rough and quick? You probably think this is a stupid question, but I really want to know and I would appreciate an answer. Not everyone wants to know only about sex. Yeah, I'm a virgin, but I don't think that's the issue. Don't be a cunt with your answer. That is, if you even answer. I bet you don't. I'm not calling you a cunt. I'm saying don't be a cunt. There's a difference. Whatever. I give up.
> **Waiting, Scott**

Alrighty then.

Listen here, you little punk: this is my house. Ask all the dumb shit you want, but don't come in here flinging the C-word and acting like I owe you shit.

You'll get a thoughtful reply. Or a verbal ass-kicking so fast your balls retract from fear. There's a difference.

Asshole.

Did I send that? No.
Did I want to? With every fiber of my filthy soul.

I dropped it here instead.

Scott is a budding serial killer. I told you this shit gets crazy. Honestly, I half-expected the next letter to be written in ransom note cutouts.

But let's be real for a second: kissing is one of the sexiest things about sex.

Kissing is everything.
It's the soft open. The trailer. The way in.

A guy can have me halfway to orgasm or halfway out the door, based entirely on how he kisses. And trust me, I'm not alone.

Women know within minutes if you're gonna be a letdown. It's primal. It's instinct.
And if you can't kiss for shit? We assume the rest of you is equally disappointing.

Yes, it goes both ways. If a chick sucks at kissing, she'll be a dead fuck too.

11

But here's the difference:
Men don't care.
They'll still fuck her.

Women?
We'll run from you so fast, you'll be crying to Mommy about your abandonment issues.

Men are from Mars, Women are from Venus.
Yeah, no shit.
I could have written that book in crayon.

Here's the truth:
If you kiss her like it's the last thing you'll ever get to do, she'll act like it's the first thing she can't live without.

But if you treat kissing like a pit stop on your way to tit-grabbing and dick-jamming, you just told her everything she needs to know.
She'll be drying up before your pants even come off.

Don't kiss like it's foreplay.
Kiss like it's the main fucking course.

Mechanics: Take it easy. I mean slooow.
There's something insanely hot about soft, barely-there kisses that brush her lips like a secret.
That kind of tease?
Wet-inducing. Bookmark that shit.
If she's squirming before your tongue even shows up, you're doing God's work.
Kiss her lips. Her cheek. Her neck.
Put your hands in her hair, on her jaw, and trace her collarbone.
Don't be afraid to just hover. Let her ache for it.

If she's leaning in, let her chase your mouth a little. Make her work for it. She'll remember you for it.

If you kiss her like you've waited your whole silly life for it?
She'll melt into your fucking hands.
That's when you feel her body go liquid, like she's about to pour herself into you.

And when you finally use your tongue, don't act like it's a shovel and her mouth is a cave.
Ease in. Let it build. Let her kiss back. Let it breathe.
If you're both gasping for air and smiling between kisses, you're on the right track.

Alternate between soft, teasing kisses and hungry, deeper ones.
Rub your lips over hers. Lick the corner of her mouth.

Then go in slow, deliberate, hot.
And for the love of all things holy and filthy, don't think "Is now a good time to go for the tit?"

FOCUS. It's not a race. It's a goddamn seduction.

Before you get cocky...
Open your eyes, genius.
Look at her while you kiss her.
That kind of eye contact? It's nuclear.

You're not just kissing her anymore. You're fucking her mind.

That's foreplay.
Where it counts.
In her mind.

Bottom line:

If you're a great kisser, she'll assume you're great at everything else. And honestly? She'll probably be right.

Some of the best sex I've ever had started with a kiss so good, I almost forgot why we were naked in the first place.

So put in the damn effort.

Make kissing a major fucking act, not just an opening one.

Kissing isn't just foreplay. It's programming.

If you do it right, she'll trust you with her whole damn body.

She'll be wet and loyal and not even know why.

... titillating tits

Let's talk tits.

Because some of you are treating them like overfilled stress balls, and frankly? That shit needs to stop.

Women are fascinated by men's fascination with tits. We're both amazed and disgusted by the way your eyes lock onto cleavage before noticing we even have a face. Let alone eye color, name, or basic human needs. Yeah. We're so pathetically needy.

And yet, while we roll our judgmental eyes and say "Ugh, men are such predictable pervs," what's our boob-obsessed reality?

Buying push-up bras.

Taping our tits together.

Wearing clingy tops to out-boob the bitch next door.

Surgically increasing that all-important cup size and swapping out what god gave us for something gravity can't even fight.

We can't count on god but we can count on a good MD. God may giveth, but Dr. Feelgood can upgrade.

We're out here grinding like Olympic athletes for the Boob Games and the gold medal.

Looking hotter than the woman who makes us feel vaguely insecure.

Why?

Because tits are magic.

They hypnotize.

They distract.

They make grown men forget what year it is. I've seen guys lose their train of thought so hard, they'd forget their own name if you flashed a nipple at the right moment.

This next bit came from a fellow webmaster, Iceman, a self-proclaimed "boob man" who sounds like he earned his PhD in titology at Hooters by day and in a strip club by night.

Is he a little meatheady? Yeah.

Is the core advice solid? Surprisingly, yes.

Let's let him try:

ICE TAKES IT

Alright guys. If you've been paying attention to TC's lessons on pussy eating, you already know the drill: if you don't lick her right, you're doomed to a lifetime of missionary sex with all the excitement of reading a credit card bill.

Now let's talk tits.

First rule: Don't just dive in like a frat boy on his first Vegas weekend with a fake ID and a loaded condom.

Get behind her.

Run your hands around her neck, across her shoulders, and down her ribs.

Take your time. Let her skin register what's coming.

Massage gently. Let her melt into it, then take her tits like you mean it.

Get a handful, respectfully. (If she's not exactly stacked, keep your goddamn mouth shut unless you want to be jerking off solo for a month.)

Caress. That means gentle, not "grab like a gorilla."

Press in on the nipples with your fingers, not your knuckles. Pinch lightly. Roll them.

Clockwise, counterclockwise. Don't just flick and stare like you found a new setting on your remote.

Now flip her around.

Bring in your mouth.

Kiss her collarbone.

Lick down the center of her chest, slow and wet.

When you get to the nipple, kiss around it. Tease. Lick in circles.

Suck it into your mouth, but lightly.

She moans? Keep going.

Here's the move:

Wet the nipple. Pull back.

Blow cool air over it. Watch it harden. Watch her shiver. That's the sound of the starter pistol, dumbass.

Now take a deep breath.

Warm your mouth.

Cup over the nipple and blow again.

Boom. Reaction achieved. Continue.

And if you're a real tit man?

Stay there for ten minutes.

Otherwise, don't fake it. She'll know.

Slide down her stomach and go back to TC's oral chapter. Double feast. Double win.

TC takes the mic back

Okay, Ice. Not bad.

Let's clean it up and finish this lesson.

Tits need attention, but more importantly, they need escalation.

Start with your fingertips.

Not your whole palm. Not both hands.

Keep it classy, not clingy. You're not kneading dough; you're waking up nerve endings she didn't even know she had.

Trace the outer curve. Work around the areola, not straight for the nipple like you're punching in for nipple duty and can't wait to clock out.

Softness creates heat.

Heat builds tension.

Tension equals control. Hold it.

Now tease. Lick slowly. Use the flat of your tongue, not the tip. Unless your tongue tip flutters like a vibrator on Red Bull.

Let it feel like worship, not maintenance.

Then pull back. Blow gently. Let her nipples harden from that contrast of wet and cool.

You're building polarity: soft and strong. Light and rough. Tender and filthy. Think of it like a playlist, but don't get stuck on repeat. Shuffle that shit.

Now suck. Just a little.

Then more.

Now nibble, but lightly. Not "biting for the sake of it" nibble. Graze your teeth over nipples. Just enough to make her twitch, arch, and squirm. Pay attention to her reactions.

That's your roadmap, fella. If she arches into you, keep going. If she pulls away, switch it up. Tits aren't a puzzle to solve—they're a conversation. Listen with your hands and mouth.

And for fuck's sake, don't stay there forever.

Unless she's into it.

In which case? Buckle up, tit boy.

If not?

Move to her neck, her lips, her stomach, her thighs, or anywhere else that keeps the momentum hot.

Let your hands stay at her breasts while your mouth explores.

Take it to the next gear.

Switch up your rhythm: slow, then fast, then slow again. Keep her guessing. Predictable is boring; unpredictable is unforgettable.

That's how you short-circuit her brain. Through her tits.

Bottom line: Tits aren't just visual bait. I've had lovers who made my whole body light up just from the way they handled my tits. And I've had others who treated them like radio dials. Static, awkward, and me begging, "Just stop, already!"

They're responsive, intelligent, erotic zones of high-voltage nerve endings, wired directly into her engine.

Handle them right?
She lights up.

Handle them wrong?
She checks out.

Do your balls matter? Tits are balls.
You treat your balls like royalty, so give her tits the same respect.

Because if you want your cock in her mouth, your hands locked on her hips, her thighs clamping down, dragging you deeper, moaning your name like a goddamn prayer—

Start with the tits.

TC Note: Iceman, I don't say this often (lie), but... *I'm wet for that.*

... the art of the handjob

I read somewhere that the average guy thinks about sex every 53 seconds. That feels like bullshit. Which means, conservatively, a guy walks around half-hard at least 10 times a day. Men don't like walking around with boners.

So they take care of it.
They whack it. Often.
If men could get frequent flyer miles for every time they jerked off, half the world would be platinum status by puberty.

And then? They write to *me* about it.

Q: I think I have a problem. I jerk off a *lot*. Like 3 times a day. One night I went 6 times just on your site. I stayed up 'til 5 a.m. and only stopped because I had work. Why am I like this? I didn't jerk off for a whole week once, but then I just... cracked. I know this is a problem, right?

A: First of all, what's the problem exactly? You're horny. You have a dick. You have WiFi. Welcome to humanity.

You asked why you're so "active" with yourself? Uhhh... because you haven't gotten laid in forever and your balls are staging a mutiny.

Six times in one night? That's not "a problem." That's just... the internet doing its job.

Unless your dick is interfering with your actual life, like blowing off work, friends, or relationships, you're fine. You're just a one-man orgy with decent stamina. Hell, you're practically a solo porn studio: lights, camera, lube.

Q: I love masturbating in front of my girlfriend. It turns us both on. But I want to spice it up. Any ideas?

Q: I've been jacking off daily. Now it's easier than dealing with my wife. I miss her, but this habit won't let go. Am I losing it?

A: Same answer for both of you: hand it over. Literally. Ask her to do it for you.

No, she won't do it "better than you." That's not the point. There's something hot, achingly hot, about your partner stumbling a little. Missing the rhythm. Gripping too soft. Too tight. Off by a second. It's unbearable. And incredible. That moment she's not sure if she's teasing you or torturing you? That's the sweet spot. The kind of frustration that makes your toes curl and your jaw clench.

TECHCHICK FACT DROP

Semen glows under blacklight because of a protein called flavin. If you want to know where the real mess is, turn off the lights and prepare to be horrified. (You're welcome.)

Want to take it next-level? Here's your playbook.

Print this. Hand it to her. No talking. Just do it.

Lay out a thick, soft blanket on the floor, next to a wall. Get completely naked. Sit with your back against the wall and your legs spread. He sits between your thighs, his back to your chest. You wrap your legs around him.

You whisper in his ear. Your voice is low, filthy. Say his name. Tell him what you want. Tell him what you did to yourself thinking about this exact moment.

Warm oil between your palms; get slippery. Let it drip down your wrists; make a mess. The wetter, the better. Slide your hands over his. Guide him with slow strokes, one hand up, the other following, alternating over the head of his cock. Don't rush. He's breathing harder. You're moaning into his neck. Let your thumb swirl over the tip, squeeze just a little tighter at the base, then loosen your grip and drag it out. Make him beg for friction, then give him just enough to keep him desperate.

Then, cover his hands with yours. Now you're jacking him off together.

The rhythm is deep and maddening. Your pussy is soaked. You're pressed skin-to-skin, and his back is sticky with sweat.

You whisper how hot it is to watch him lose control, to feel every twitch and pulse as he teeters right on the edge. Tell him you want to see his face when he loses it. Tell him you want every drop, every shudder, every filthy sound.

Stay in his ear the whole time. Say the kind of shit you can't unsay.

When he cums, he collapses back into you. You hold him. Kiss his neck. Slide out from behind. Then kneel between his legs. Look him in the eye.

And clean. Him. Up.
With your mouth.
Every drop.
You swallow and smile.
Hold his cock in your mouth for a second longer; let him feel just how much you love the taste of him. Look up, make eye contact. Let him watch you savor every drop.

Deep breath.

If you're not a little lightheaded, go back and read that again. Wipe off, sip something cold, and let's dive back in.

... Q&A: Foreplay Overload

Some people think foreplay is optional. Some people also think socks with sandals are sexilicious. I don't listen to those people.

Q. My partner says she wants more foreplay, but I feel like I'm already doing plenty. How much is enough?

A. How do I put this? You foreplay her until she cums. For most women, "enough" is about three times more than whatever you're doing now. Five minutes? Try fifteen. And don't just clock-watch; make it count. If she's not melting into the mattress or clawing at the sheets, you're not done. Simple as that. If you're treating foreplay like a warm-up lap, she's treating you like a pit stop. The goal is to make her feel desired, relaxed, and completely focused on sensation.

Q. Is dirty talk actually a turn-on, or does it just sound awkward?

A. Dirty talk is like tequila: a little goes a long way, and too much will have you waking up with regrets. But done right? It's nuclear. Don't overthink it.

Start with a whisper, not a script. Say what you want to do to her or what she's doing to you, and mean it. If you sound like you're reading porn subtitles, stop. If you make her laugh, roll with it. Humor is hot. If she starts giggling, you're not losing; she's letting her guard down. That's foreplay for the brain.

True story: I once had a guy whisper, "I want to ravish you like a Viking." I lost it. We both did. Still got laid.
Moral: If you're going to fail, fail with flair.

Q. I love foreplay, but sometimes I feel like I want it instead of sex, not just as the lead-in. Is that weird? (Also, I'm a woman. I know you probably don't hear from us as much, but some of us are just as into sex as the horny dudes out there.)

A. Not weird, wise. The whole idea that sex has to end in penetration is a guy myth. Sometimes (read: often), a good tongue and two fingers can do more than a full-on fuck. If you're feeling fully satisfied from foreplay alone, just say so.

That's not a failure to "finish." That *is* the finish. Don't downplay it to make him feel like he closed the deal. If he pouts because you didn't let him finish, remind him: you did. And that's the only score that matters tonight.

Q. I've heard it said that foreplay doesn't start in the bedroom. I honestly don't understand what that means. I hope it doesn't mean I have to be foreplaying her all day or something just to get laid in the evening?

A. Hell yes. Some of the best foreplay starts hours before you even see each other. Send a filthy text. Foreplay is a slow burn. If you're not making her squirm in public just thinking about what you'll do later, you're missing half the fun. Whisper something nasty in her ear at dinner. Brush your hand over her thigh when no one's watching. Build the anticipation so by the time you're alone, she's already halfway to the finish line.

True story: I once got so worked up by a string of dirty texts that the second he walked through the door, we didn't even make it to the bed.

25

My fantasy: slow seduction.

My reality: butt-ass naked, getting railed over the kitchen counter, eyes locked on a grease stain and not giving a single fuck. 10/10, would recommend.

... A Day in the Life: Tits, Clicks & Chaos (Foreplay)

The start of my workday as a smut webmistress? It's a lot like foreplay:

Starts with good intentions.

Sets the mood.

Feels pretty damn great once I'm into it.

And if it goes sideways, everything that follows is probably going to suck. Just like bad foreplay, a rough start can ruin the whole damn session.

Like any job, mine has its perks... and it's "fuck this day, I'm getting drunk" moments.

The Good:

I work from home in shorts, a t-shirt, no bra, two-day-old panties and zero judgment. Living the "fuck dress codes" dream.

I'm the boss. I make the rules. I break them daily, religiously, with zeal.

I can upload the perfect hardcore fuck pic, write copy, cook pasta, and fold towels—sometimes all at once.

Sleeping till noon and working till 4 a.m.? Approved by management (hi, me).

I get to cash checks that prove I'm not just some degenerate with a Wi-Fi fetish.

The Bad:
I always look like a degenerate with a Wi-Fi fetish.

Truth: Nothing says 'living the dream' like getting paid for making strangers horny in your pajamas.

My boss gives zero direction, probably has no clue what the fuck she's doing, and is a cranky bitch most of the time.

That laundry? Still in the basket. That pasta? Cold. But hey, I found a perfect anal GIF. Priorities.
If multitasking was an Olympic sport, I'd have a gold medal in orgasm math and carb loading.

I haven't slept in years. My bed is twelve feet from my "office," and my brain keeps crawling toward the monitor like it's lit with dopamine and filthy little secrets.

The bank teller squints at my deposit and says,
"Um... this check is from Cocksuckers, LTD?"
I nod like a professional: "Yes. Business is booming."

The Ugly:
Some days I forget what month it is, answer the door half-dressed, and wonder why the UPS guy lobs my precious packages like he's seen shit and wants no part of it.

And some days, it's harder to start than others.
You open the laptop, stare at the blinking cursor, and suddenly your brain is a dried-up clit that hasn't seen friction in weeks.

No ideas. No spark. No lube.

Foreplay isn't just part of sex. It's the art of beginning. If you can't get yourself in the mood, how the hell are you going to get anyone else there? The soft, slow tease into momentum. And when it's missing? Everything else feels forced.

So you wait. You scroll. You lie to yourself: "I'll just check traffic stats." "Maybe one forum post." "This is research." But really, you're hoping something—anything—will make you want to touch the damn keyboard again.

And that's just Monday. Wait till you see what happens when the server crashes, my cat decides to plant his ass on my keyboard (visualization won't help), and I must explain to my accountant why "ButtStuffBonanza" is a legitimate business expense.

Eating Pussy & Clitoral Confusion

... clit happens

A clit isn't a joystick. It's a live wire in lace panties. — TechChick

If there's one non-negotiable to being legendary in bed, it's this: earn your PhD in pussy eating. Other degrees won't get you half as far. You can fuck up plenty else: the position, the rhythm, the order of operations. But if your mouth game is weak, too fast, too clueless, too damn aggressive, you're going down in flames before she ever makes a sound that matters.

The clit is everything. It's not a side dish. It's not an à la carte add-on. It's the goddamn main course. If you skip it, you might as well order takeout and eat alone. Don't believe me? Ask any woman who's had to fake her way through a jackhammer fuckfest that left her clenching her teeth and praying to a god she doesn't believe in for it to just motherfucking end.

Want to be unforgettable? Eat pussy like your next orgasm depends on it. Because hers absolutely does.

Don't Do This Shit.
If your first move is fast, rough, or frantic—borderline freakish—she's either pretending to enjoy it… or there is no "or."
She's faking it. Period.

Ignore Feedback That's Telling You Everything
If you're not paying attention to how she's reacting, her sounds (silence = no bueno), breathing, and body language, you're not eating pussy. You're licking blindly. Stop guessing. Watch her. Feel her. React.

The Alphabet Move
This one needs to die already. You know, the one where you're supposed to "write the alphabet" with your tongue? Not only is it awkward, but how the hell are you supposed to stay turned on while mentally reciting your ABCs? Besides, random letters don't feel good, dammit. They feel confusing, inconsistent, and weird. You want rhythm, repetition, and intent. Most women just want you to find what works and stay the fuck there.

Treat Every Woman the Same

There's no universal cheat code (like there is with blowjobs). What worked on your ex might be a total disaster here. Ask what she likes. Listen. Learn. Not a talker? Watch what works. Then do that. Over and over. Again and again.

Get Bored and Zone Out

If you're not into it, don't bother. If you're down there thinking about fantasy football, she can tell. If you're not into her, she feels it. Enthusiasm really is the secret sauce. Don't fake it; either mean it or skip it.

Treat Porn Like a Pussy Playboo

Lizard tongue? Motorboating? Throat growls? Stop. Porn is not a tutorial. Real-life women want real pleasure. Yes, there's some complexity down there, but that's no excuse for throwing everything at it to see what sticks. Just no.

Why it Matters

The majority of women don't orgasm from penetration alone. And honestly, I say "majority" generously. Truth is, I don't know a single truth-telling woman who cums just from being fucked.

For the doubters, there are plenty of stats to back me up: only about 18% of women climax from penetration alone, while the rest need clitoral stimulation to get there.

See? Even the so-called experts with credentials confirm what I already knew (and frankly, I think that 18% is inflated). It's the clit. It's always been the clit. Period.

Worship it. Prioritize it. Understand that when you put her pleasure first, everything changes.

We love your cocks. But we need your tongues.

Use them like they matter, and the filthy doors to heaven swing open.

Now, you can't exactly fuck a clit. Not unless your dick is shaped like a thumb drive and vibrates like a high-end sex toy. Which means you're going down. With your mouth. With intention. With tongue and lips and the kind of god-tier focus usually reserved for bomb techs and brain surgeons.

Yes, you can finger it. Yes, toys can play backup. But nothing, nothing replaces a warm mouth and a wet tongue used with skill, patience, and dirty devotion. That's what makes her twitch and moan and grip the sheets like she's bracing for liftoff.

Let's also be real here.

You want more blowjobs? Want to fuck her in the ass? Want to jizz all over her face, dress her in latex, handcuff her to the radiator and call it Tuesday? Then get her off first. With your mouth. Do it well. Do it often. If you give her head that sends her into orbit, she'll want to do all that filthy shit with you. Not out of obligation, but because you made her feel like a goddess. It's chemistry. It's confidence. It's the difference between a one-time fuck and a lifelong obsession.

Here's your new mantra: Her first. Get her off before you fuck her, and what you'll slide into is a tight, dripping, pulse-wrapped gift from the sex gods. You're welcome.

Now, burn this into your worldview: Her pussy smells like jasmine, tastes like strawberries and cream, and looks like modern art (eh, give it a try).

Now let's get to work, gentlemen...

... tongue first, questions later

> ### TECHCHICK FACT DROP
> The clitoris has over 8,000 nerve endings, twice as many as the penis. Handle with care (and enthusiasm).

Prelude to Worship

This isn't just technique. It's tension. It's anticipation so thick you could lick it off her thighs. You want her soaking, not just wet. Unraveling, not just interested. She needs to ache for your mouth like it's her last goddamn request. If you're not both vibrating with want, you're not ready. Now you're ready.

The Descent

She's spread out in front of you. Skin flushed. Thighs slick. Breath shaking. You hover over her like you're about to deliver salvation. Your hands barely graze the inside of her knees. Your mouth drags up her thigh. Slow, cruel, deliberate. Goosebumps rise. You breathe her in. Musky, sweet, dizzying. She tastes like heat and surrender.

Don't ruin it by charging in. Kiss her everywhere but where she needs it. Let your mouth wander. Tongue warm, lips open, lazy and wet. Trace her hipbones. Dip into the crease where thigh meets pelvis. Leave a trail of spit. Blow gently. Watch her shiver.

Skip the slick heat between her legs. Brush past it like you didn't notice the cream pooling at her ass, even though it's already hijacked your brain.

If her hands are in your hair, pulling, ignore her. Just long enough to make her squirm. Let her grind against nothing. Make her beg with her hips before you give her anything.

Mouth Open

She's parted and arched. Breathing like she's trying not to plead. Go in slow. Not the clit, not yet. Start with her outer lips. Inner lips. Kiss them like they're sacred. Lick the opening. Let her watch you savor it. That's her porn: you, loving her. Now stiffen your tongue. Slide it inside. Deep. Slow. Circular. Stay until she forgets you have hands. This isn't a warm-up. This is its own kink. It's raw. Intimate. Feral. She won't know if she's going to cum, cry, or crush your skull between her thighs just to survive it.

Flatten your tongue. Drag it up her slit. Taste everything. Swirl inside her. Let her ride your face until her thighs start to shake.

Technique: The Real Shit

Slow tongue. Soft tongue. Light pressure. Rhythmic movement. If you're licking like a windshield wiper on meth, stop. No woman has ever come from chaos.

She'll tell you everything with her body, breath, moans, the way her hands grip your scalp. Watch. Listen. Respond. Don't push. Don't rush. Let her unfold.

At Last... The Clit

You hover just above her clit, so close she can feel the heat of your breath but not your tongue. You flick your tongue out, barely brushing her, then pull away. You blow a stream of warm air, watching her clit pulse and swell. When you finally close your mouth around her, you suck gently, then harder, flicking your tongue in tight, relentless circles. Her hands are in your hair, her thighs locked around your ears, and her voice breaking as she begs for more.

Suck, Don't Just Lick

Suction is everything. Seal your lips. Suck in rhythm. Tongue moving between pulses. No improvising. Lock in. Steady pressure. That's how she explodes. If she's writhing, thrusting—that's not discomfort. That's escape velocity. You hang the fuck on.

Fingers: Optional but Glorious

If your lips are locked on, fingers can unlock the rest. Two fingers. Wet. Curved upward. Sync your rhythm. Slide in slowly. Stroke with intention. Touch her nipples. Tease her ass. Don't overwhelm. Every move should earn its place. Just keep it deliberate. She's giving you the blueprint with every breath, every twitch. Don't crowd her body with noise. Make every move count. Every breath, every shift, it's a signal. Don't perform. Respond.

She's not a stage, you're not auditioning; this is a duet, and she's writing the sheet music with her body.

The Aftershock

Her body stiffens. Back arches. Thighs lock around your face. Her nails find your scalp. You do not stop. Her orgasm stops the second you do. Ride it out. Ease up if she squirms but stay present. Stay with her. She'll push you off when she's done. Until then? Hold. Your. Ground.

Final Touch

When it's over, don't rinse your mouth. Don't act like you licked a subway pole. Crawl up her body. Kiss her deeply. Let her taste herself. Whisper in her ear, "That's what you do to me." Let her feel it in her chest. In her gut. Make her crave the next time before she can even breathe.

The mouth is the dick. Use it like it's your million-dollar job. And baby, business will be booming.

... a pussy has nine lives

*Your pussy isn't fragile. It's just
under-lubed and over-apologized
for. — TechChick*

Some women worry about their pussies far too much. Like it's going
to break if they fuck too often. Stretch out like an old sock. Or develop
some sort of wear and tear from a husband with an overactive dick.

It still amazes me how little some women know about their own bodies.
Me? I want to know everything. And I think that should be the norm.

But every now and then, I get a letter like this:

> **Dear TechChick,**
>
> I am desperate for your advice. I'm a happily married wom-
> an of four years. My husband is great in every way. I have no
> complaints. Except one.
>
> He wants sex all the time. Every day. Sometimes more
> than once.
>
> And here's the problem: my pussy can't handle it. I'm sore,
> I'm raw, and I'm tired. Don't get me wrong, I love him and
> I love our sex. It's exciting and erotic and everything I hoped
> it would be.
>
> It's just the frequency. Please tell me how to keep my hus-
> band happy without wrecking my vagina in the process. My
> pussy can't handle it.
> **— Jackie R.**

Who says pussies can't handle the heat?

Dear Jackie,

Don't sweat it, a pussy has nine lives. Let me explain. You probably haven't heard of the Houston 500 or the Houston 620, but I promise your husband has.

No, this isn't NASCAR. We're talking porn, and pussy. Houston was a porn star who made a name for herself by letting 500 men (and later, 620) fuck her in one giant, highly choreographed session.

It was a publicity stunt, a business move, and a massive gangbang rolled into one, and yes, the whole thing was taped and sold by the truckload.

The setup? Surprisingly orderly. The men were pre-screened for STDs. Each had one minute to do the deed. No cumming on her face. No chaos. Just a naked woman on a table, displayed like a holiday turkey while hundreds of dudes lined up to take a turn.

The shoot took around 18 hours, factoring in piss breaks and make-up retouches, and was edited into a two-hour feature film that sold millions.

Her skin must've been slick with lube and sweat, every muscle quivering beneath the weight of the next man in line.

One-minute fucks. And reportedly? 18 cases of K-Y Jelly.

If she can take 500 men in under a day, I think the average woman can handle a couple of enthusiastic rounds with her husband, especially if she learns from the pros: keep it quick, keep it lubed, and give your pussy the recovery it needs to bounce back.

About a month later, Houston volunteered for labia surgery. She filmed it, sold it, even auctioned the tissue in Lucite like an X-rated trophy

And yes, she filmed that too. Sold another shitload of copies. Being the most ambitious money-seeker in porn, she even auctioned off the excised tissue, encased in Lucite, like some X-rated trophy. I shit you not. Gross? Maybe. Fucking awesome? Absolutely. That's straight-up legend behavior.

Bottom line: Your pussy isn't broken. It's just tired. Keep it wet, pace yourself, and remind your husband that even Ferrari need pit stops. If anyone tries to tell you otherwise, remind them: Houston took 500 in a day and still cashed her check. Your vagina's got nine lives, and then some.

— **TechChick**

... Q&A: Pussy Fails

Some men treat going down like it's radioactive. Others act like it's just an optional side dish. What the hell makes pussy so scary and so unimportant at the same time?

Q. My husband won't go down on me. He did it twice while we were dating for five months and only three times during our eight-month marriage. I've asked, pleaded, and even begged.

I always give him blowjobs, and our sex life is decent, except for the part where I never get oral. He'll finger me sometimes, but even that's rare. He won't give a real reason, just "I don't feel like it" or "What's the big deal?"

And every time I bring it up, he gets defensive and we end up not having sex at all for weeks. I'm sick of this. I feel like I'm entitled to some oral pleasure, especially since I'm so willing to do anything for him in bed. What do I do?

A. Don't walk. RUN. This selfish bastard has no plans to change, and honestly? He doesn't deserve that mouth of yours. There are plenty of men out there who love giving head and don't treat it like a chore.

And let's just file this under "lessons learned": if he only went down on you twice in five months of dating, why the fuck did you marry him?

That's not a man; that's a red flag with a penis. Go find someone whose lips make you melt, not recoil.

Q. I want to go down on my girlfriend, but I'm honestly nervous I'll suck at it (not in the good way). I've read stuff online but everyone says something different. I'm afraid I'll do it wrong and she'll be disappointed. What if I just can't figure out what she likes?

A. First of all, thank you for not being one of the "oral sex is icky" Neanderthals. That said, get over yourself. She doesn't want perfection; she wants enthusiasm.

If you care, if you're paying attention, if you keep asking what she likes and actually listen, you're already ahead of 80% of the population. Now get in there and make some mistakes.

It's not surgery. It's sex. She'll appreciate the effort, especially if you don't pout when she gives you notes.

Q. I'm a decent guy in bed, but oral has always tripped me up. I can't tell if she's enjoying it or just waiting for it to be over. What should I be looking for?

A. Let's make this simple. Moaning = good. Breathing harder = good. Pulling your head closer = very good. Laying there silent like she's astral projecting out of boredom? Not so good.

If she arches toward you, keep doing what you're doing. If she suddenly shifts, sighs, or goes still, well my friend, you just lost the signal.

Think of her body like a live GPS. It's telling you exactly where to go; you just keep missing the damn turn. Pay attention. Adjust. Don't be the guy who gets lost and still refuses to ask for directions. No one likes that guy.

Q. Let's see if you can help me. I'm 21/m and have been seeing this 35/f for the past month. I've learned a lot from her in bed, but I really want to satisfy her even more. I already make her cum at least three times when we fuck, mostly with my tongue, but I'm wondering what else I can do to help her orgasm more?

A. Oh, quit your whining, you show-off.

... A Day in the Life: Of Clits

Sometimes a person doesn't want to give oral sex, they'd rather just lay there and get serviced themselves.

My job is like that. There's a never-ending shitlist of tasks that need doing for the "greater good," even though many days, I'd rather kick back and let my little porn world burn. That's how it goes in the smut business: everyone wants someone else to handle the mess, and preferably for just-barely minimum wage and maximum porn perks.

I've burned through more assistants than I can count. Every newbie thinks they've hit the jackpot: work from home in their boxers while scratching their nuts, porn on tap. Doritos in lap. But after a day or two, reality sets in.

Suddenly, they're demanding triple pay, threatening mutiny, or just sending a one-liner resignation: "FUCK YOU." I've been through a shit ton of assistants. Currently I am assistantless.

Meanwhile, my own clit is still waiting to be worshipped—another day, another digital chore.

The job I always want to delegate but never can? The dreaded "site sweep."
It's the digital assistant's version of toilet-scrubbing: unsexy, thankless, and essential. Every damn page has to be checked to make sure it still links to actual porn and not banner farms, popup console hell, or worse, some scat-filled horror show.

Some webmasters are straight-up trolls who swap out your "innocent" galleries the second you link them. Next thing you know you're pointing at foot-fetish midgets, piss shows, or worse. If you don't keep up, your site turns into a graveyard of dead ends and pissed-off site visitors.

Performing the "site sweep" is a shitty and treacherous job because you might find any number of things that either turn your stomach or piss you off to no end. It's not just tedious, it's traumatic.

Miss a sweep, and all your hard-earned traffic goes poof, and just for funsies, a fuckload of mega-angry emails. In essence, we're talking about porn customer service at its most violent.

Myth: once you set a link, it stays true to its word. Reality: links lie, so always double-check before you click.

Just like you wouldn't skip checking for dead links, don't ignore dead zones on her body. Spread your attention across her entire clit hood, inner lips, and perineum (that spot between her pussy and her asshole).

One time, I actually found an assistant who stayed for two whole weeks. I was living the dream. He was doing a great job and seemed totally at peace with the daily shitlist. I was in employer heaven. And then, out of nowhere, came the resignation bomb:

Yo TC,

I'm really sorry to do this to ya babe but uh I have a little problem here. Not just a little problem, it's a full-blown crisis! It's my wife.

First a little background on me that I didn't think was relevant at the time you hired me. I'm what I guess you would call a porn freak. Not just online porn but dirty books and videos and all the men's mags.

Anyway, about eight months ago my wife found my whole collection and hit the roof. She threw every bit of it out and threatened to leave me if she ever caught me with that "trash" again. I love her and it's not worth losing her over so I promised her that was the end of it.

Then you came along. Or I should say the job came along. It sounded perfect to me (working from home in my boxers and looking at porn all day while scratching my nuts and getting paid for it, no offense). Anyway, I figured I could hide it from my wife while she was at work, only I got caught yesterday.

She walked in on me unexpectedly while I was checking one of your links that just happened to go to a gallery of pics with foot fucking midgets as the theme.

As she came in to take a closer look I closed the window immediately and I thought I got away with it but up popped one of those fucking consoles showing another gallery with a cowboy pissing on a blonde transvestite amazon freak of a dude in six-inch stilettos.

I closed that one too, but the popups came so fast and with worse and worse content, if you can even imagine.

Jesus, what kind of webmasters do you do business with anyway that submit that shit to you? Anyway, by the time I got all the shit closed down I was left with one lonely window that we both stared at what seemed like forever, that being a 300 pound, 60-year-old "performer" in pigtails who was getting triple penetrated in an asshole that I swear was the size of a tuba.

To make a long story short, the rest of the day was a fucking nightmare and my explanation of, "honey, I SWEAR I'm getting paid real money to look at this shit!!!" didn't begin to cut it. I'm in deep shit, probably headed for divorce, and I don't blame you TC, but I QUIT!
Wish me luck, Jerry

TC Note: this is the longest resignation letter my brain-weary brain has ever received. Why not just say "FUCK YOU" and be done with it, Jerry?

I knew it was too good to be true. I do wish him luck, though. Anyone out there looking for a job?

Oh, and for the curious: before Jerry quit, he did yank the infamous link. So don't bother searching for the 300-pound, 50-year-old pornstar in pigtails getting triple penetrated in her tuba-sized asshole. I know you were about to.

And that's just Tuesday. Wait till you see what happens when I spend all afternoon deleting pop-ups, only to realize my new "assistant" was actually my neighbor's teenage son hacking my Wi-Fi for free porn, and I have to explain to my hosting company why "ClitQuest" is trending in their abuse reports.

The Penis Files

... in the beginning, there was the dick

A clit is patient. A dick is standing there like, "Woman, this is a boner emergency." — TechChick

Before there was fire, before there was the wheel, there was a dick throbbing in the dark, standing at attention, demanding to be noticed, and generally making a spectacle of itself.

Some men rank blowjobs right up there with screwing. Those men are clearly getting their dicks sucked by someone who knows what they're doing. Lucky bastards.

Whatever your feelings, one thing's true: giving a great blowjob is an art. It takes experience, knowledge of the genitalia being serviced, and a strong desire to actually make your partner feel good.

Tip: Keep your lips loose and your jaw flexible. Think gentle swirl, not death grip.

TECHCHICK FACT DROP

Erections last because blood gets in and can't get out, literally. That's why a hard-on over 4 hours is a medical emergency. If you ever wanted a reason to brag at the ER, "I was just too hard for too long" is as good as it gets.

For men, getting head isn't just a sexual perk or a warm-up. It's a litmus test. It says, "Do you want me? Are you into me? Do you even give a shit about my pleasure?"

The only qualification to receive one? A heartbeat. Hell, sometimes not even that.

Unfortunately, too many women treat it like a chore. An optional side job she might accept once a year—if the planets align, it's his birthday, or she's bracing for divorce papers. My inbox proves the damage:

Dear TechChick,

What does a man have to do to get his dick sucked every once in a while? My wife acts like she hates it, like she's doing me a huge favor every time I ask.

Forget her initiating it. Forget swallowing, you'd think I asked her to take a bullet. When we were dating, she was all about it. That was two years ago. Two years to the day I did the dumbest thing I've ever done: say "I do" to a woman who would never suck my dick again. I don't really want to call her a bitch, but seriously, what a bitch!

— Dying Here

Dear Dying,

That hostility you're feeling? Justified. Your wife is what I call a fake sucker, a woman who acted like she enjoyed giving head up to the point she found some poor male sucker to meet her at the altar.

There are only two kinds of women when it comes to blowjobs: real suckers (they love giving pleasure), and fake suckers (they use it as bait, then act like it's a war crime).

Real suckers keep it up long after the honeymoon phase. Maybe they love the act; maybe they just love seeing their partner lose his mind. You can't fake wanting to please someone. If she's not into it, you can't coach it into existence.

So what do you do if you've got a fake sucker on your hands? Talk to her, straight up. Tell her how much it means to you, how good it feels, and that you want this in your sex life. If she's still unresponsive, you've got a decision to make:

Live with it and accept it.

Get your blowjobs elsewhere.

Move on and find a real sucker.

I cringe to say: "Life is too short." Buttt... life is too short!

— **TechChick**

Women supremely underestimate how important blowjobs are to a man's happiness, just as a woman might say, "If he'd only do that one little thing, it would make such a big difference." For men, that "little thing" is often oral.

It's not "just sex." It's not about being spoiled; it's about feeling wanted. It's connection. It's devotion. It's mental health care with a happy ending. And swallowing? It's goddamn important.

Not because it's some porn trope, but because it says everything without a single word: I want you. I accept you. I'm not grossed out by you.

Myth: blowjobs are a bonus.
Reality: they're love letters written in saliva.

For my ladies, let's flip the script so you can really feel this one.

He's going down on you. You're cumming. And right at that moment, he pulls back to dodge it.

Or worse, he stays for the ride... then spits it out like you just attempted murder by poison.

Really sit with that.

Motherfucking ouch.

If you truly can't bring yourself to swallow, fine, but don't rob him of intimacy.

Let him cum in your mouth, then let it spill back out over his dick while you keep moving, licking, stroking.

It still feels connected. It still feels like a gift.

But if you can swallow? Swallow. That's the pinnacle.

A green light. A trust fall. A standing ovation, all rolled into one gulp.

This isn't me just pulling something out of my ass (although, it's been known to happen. Literally).

Research backs this up. Swallowing gets coded psychologically as enthusiasm, desire, connection.

And when it doesn't happen? Some men feel rejected, even if they won't admit it.

Swallowing is the ultimate finish—a climactic yes to the whole encounter. If it's not your thing, fine. Just don't act shocked when he starts writing sonnets about the last girl who did.

So yeah, suck his dick more.

And swallow.

Just fucking swallow. It's not battery acid.

... in the end, there was the dick

If men could date their own dicks, most of them would. They already spend half their lives obsessing over them. The other half is just logistics. — *TechChick*

Some women treat giving head like a favor. Others? Like a calling. Men, don't give up hope. Even if my inbox is full of "how do I get my wife to suck my dick?" I also get plenty from women desperate to know: "How do I give him the best blowjob he's ever had?"

Every woman should know how to give a proper blowjob. It's a rite of passage.

Every part of a blowjob should feel like a seamless, sensual flow, one continuous, escalating experience. No disjointed moves. Just connection, rhythm, and heat. Hot as fuck.

So, let's get down to the real shit: technique.

Slow. The Fuck. Down.

Confidence is hot. Being truly present is hotter. Let him feel that you don't have to do this, you want to do this. Be in charge. You're not clocking in for a chore; you're building a bomb. Every moment should drip with intention.

Start with your eyes. Look at him like you're about to do a very wicked thing. Huge turn-on. Then break eye contact and work your way down, teasing, slow, and deliberate. Touch him everywhere except his cock. Run your fingers up his thighs, across his stomach, and over his hips. Let your breath ghost across his skin.

Then kiss him. Really kiss him. Take your time. Let your mouth drag down his neck, chest, stomach, pelvis, and inner thighs. Linger. Lick. Let your tongue send messages your hands can't. Make him wait for it.

Teasing isn't just delay. It's control. It's telling his brain: "Not yet." Anticipation is foreplay.
The longer you take, the more he'll hate you in all the best possible ways.

Spit. Drool. Slobber. Make it Obscene.

Now hover. Let your lips brush his skin. Then almost touch him, but don't. Let your tongue tease his thighs, his balls, and the base of his shaft. Let him feel your breath before he ever feels your mouth. When he's practically begging...

Take him in. With a mouthful of saliva, make an "O" shape with your lips and slide down over the head, then further if you can. Let the drool flow. Keep your lips over your teeth making a cushion as you go down. Use suction on the way up. Relax your jaw on the way down. Then do it again, slower. And again, deeper. Let the slobber puddle. Alternate with licking, swirling, sucking. Everything in slow motion.

Hands + Mouth = Meltdown.

Your mouth's not doing this solo. Hands amplify everything. When your hand and mouth move as one, you overwhelm his nervous system in the best possible way.

Grip the base of his shaft firmly. As your mouth slides down, your hand follows. Your mouth and hand should meet and move as one, creating a seamless, wet, tight tunnel of sensation. Twist your wrist back and forth as you slide. Add a swirl with your tongue. Stroke, twist, tease.

Use your other hand to cup his balls like they're fine china. Gently stroke the area between his balls and his ass (the perineum). It's a nerve-ending jackpot. And it keeps the stimulation going even while your mouth switches things up.

Rhythm and Nearing the Brink.

Find your rhythm. As he gets more worked up, increase the speed and pressure, but don't go jackhammer. Listen for his breathing, his moans, and his body tensing. That's your cue to fuck with his very being and back down. Slow it down. Blend your moves.

Take him to the brink and back. Slide from sucking to licking to circling his tip. Flatten your tongue and lick from the base of his cock all the way up. Swirl the head. Then finally, have mercy, and take him deep.

Use eye contact while you're working. It's intimate. Primal. And it keeps the connection unbearably strong.

Finish Strong. Don't Rush the Ending.
Stay steady as he gets close. When he's about to cum, this is the moment to keep your rhythm and pressure consistent. No abrupt changeups now. Do. Not. Stop.

Use your hand to keep him fully encased, even if you can't take him all the way. Want to draw it out? Loop your thumb and forefinger around the base of his cock, like keeping air in a balloon, then ease up and start again.

With practice, you can edge him three, four times, and the explosion will make him feel like you yanked his soul out through his dick and didn't give it back.

Aftercare matters.
Once he finishes, keep your mouth or hand on him for several more seconds. Let him ride the aftershocks. Stay with him. Suck through it.

Swallow.
Let him shake. Then pull off slowly and kiss your way back up his body. This makes the whole experience feel complete and connected, like syncing his body, brain, and balls in perfect fucking harmony.

Congratulations. You didn't just blow him. You baptized him.

Happy Sucking, TC

... the unvarnished suck

If you're not leaving him wrecked and a little scared, what's the point? — TechChick

We'd barely made it out of the last chapter alive, and now you want to really suck a dick like you mean it? Good. Because this part isn't about tips or tricks. It's not about swirl patterns or jaw angles. It's about being unhinged. Raw. Filthy. Hungry.

This is what it looks like when you don't plan it. When you don't ask. When the craving hits and you just fucking do it. Who says blowjobs need planning?

...were headed to the bar for a drink, then dinner. He was driving his big-ass, super-extended, thingamajiggy of a Ford Expedition. We stopped at a red light. Busy intersection. Lots of traffic.

I leaned over and kissed him on the cheek, and then it hit me: *I'm gonna blow his fucking mind.*

I unzipped his pants, which was a challenge. SUVs aren't designed for filth and consoles are the enemy, but I managed. He glanced over, confused.

"What are you doing?"

The light turned green. I told him, "Relax and drive."

And I reached in and grabbed his cock. He was already hard. The tip was wet.

I licked it.

He moaned. "I can't do this while I'm driving."

"You don't have to do anything," I said. "Just drive."

I circled my tongue around the head. He squirmed. Moaned again. I wrapped my hand around the base, stroking slowly while my tongue stayed focused up top, teasing, wet, deliberate.

More red lights. More traffic. He couldn't fully relax.

But I didn't stop.

He kept saying "Oh, shit..." and trying to shift in his seat. I started sucking just the head while still stroking, and eventually, his hand found the back of my head. He moaned my name. Traffic blurring, lights changing, he was barely driving.

"Wait," he said.

I didn't.

I sucked harder.

He was stiff as hell, but tense, twitchy, too much stimulation, not enough stillness. I eased up. Backed off. Just gentle licks and slow strokes, trying to soothe him. Wet, lazy tongue up and down his shaft like a slow dance.

His hand slid under my shirt. Found my nipples. I moaned. Outside, the noise of honking and engines and motion kept building, but in that SUV, it was just wet sounds and breath and pressure.

Eventually, we parked.

He left the engine running and leaned his seat back. I went in again, this time with intent. Tongue, suction, rhythm. I rubbed his balls through his jeans. My head moved up and down with that steady pace I knew he loved.

He moaned hard. Said my name. Groaned.

And came. Hard.

He shoved my head down on him, lost in it. I swallowed, still moving on him slowly.

"Stop," he begged. Too much.

I didn't. Not right away.

He had to pull my head off him.

I licked the last bit off his tip, zipped him up, and smiled:

"Let's go."

He looked so wrecked wobbling into that bar. I was slutty-proud. Like, gold-medal, mouth-still-tingling proud.

... deepthroating: don't die trying

Deepthroating isn't a party trick. It's surrender, kink, and performance art. If you want it to be. If you don't? Don't do it. But if you do? Buckle the fuck up.
— *TechChick*

Some women are terrified of it. Others treat it like a blowjob black belt. Me? I've got mixed feelings. But I'll tell you this: nothing blows up my inbox faster than even mentioning deepthroating. So here we go...

Dear TC,

How important is it to DT (deepthroat) a guy when giving him a blowjob? I think I give pretty good blowjobs. I've never had any complaints but I feel like I'm not taking enough of him. Is this something I should work on or is it unimportant if the blowjob is good overall? Waiting for your answer.
Thank you! — Candice

Dear Candice,

If he's getting off and you're both having a good time, you don't have a thing to worry about. Deepthroating isn't some mandatory blowjob requirement. It's not the gold standard. It's just one way to dial things up, and only if you want to. Some guys get off on the visual, some love the feeling, and some just like the idea of being buried that deep. But none of that matters if it feels like a chore to you.

If you're curious, try it. If it turns you on to push that limit, explore it. But if the whole thing stresses you out or makes you gag in a bad way, skip it. A good blowjob isn't measured in inches. It's measured in attention, rhythm, confidence.

So yes, it's something you can work on, but only if it turns you on. Not because you think you're falling short.
— **TC**

The very first time I posted a blowjob tip on my website, I added a little teaser at the end: "Next week's tip: Hmmm... I think I'll do one on deepthroating... whatcha think?" I got 138 emails in two days basically begging for it.

So yeah. It's a thing.

But let me say this upfront: deepthroating is overrated.

Guys who've never experienced it think it's the holy grail, because, hell, the idea is usually hotter than the reality. But ask someone who's actually been deepthroated, and they'll tell you: a really good blowjob is just as hot, sometimes even better than a lung-choking DT any day.

When a woman knows what she's doing, it almost doesn't matter how many inches are in her mouth. It's about pressure, rhythm, spit, and enthusiasm. If his dick is wrapped in wet, hot sensation—mouth, hands, tongue, lips—he's in heaven. Still... one male friend of mine made a solid point:

"What deepthroating is really good for is the visual."

Yeah. I couldn't argue with that one.

The Mental Game.
Here's what you need to know: deepthroating isn't just a skill. It's a decision. It takes practice, relaxation, and a willingness to be a little... unhinged.

If you're the one doing it, don't do it for him. Do it because you're curious. Because you want to push yourself. Because you want to feel him slide into a part of your body you don't usually sexualize. Not feeling that energy? Skip it.

Still here? Okay, let's break this down.

Prep & Practice.
Start with a dildo. Yes, absofuckinglutely. Why? Because he's going to get way too excited to sit still for a blowjob rehearsal. Practicing solo means no dick-thrashing, no premature applause, no unattractive gagging, just you, a mirror, and your own damn tempo.

That gag reflex? No joke. It's the main roadblock. The trick? Swallowing.

Practicing how to swallow with something in your mouth (you know, like you do at the dentist) helps minimize the reflex. Take in a little, swallow. A little more, swallow. Visualize how you have to swallow with your mouth open at the dentist: tongue lolling, suction tube fighting for its life, hygienist telling you to 'relax your throat' (yeah, fuck off, lady) while holding a medieval metal hook. Same energy, minus the crinkly paper bib and random wonky mouth suctioning.

Tongue & Throat.
The tongue is the next obstacle. It needs to get out of the way.

Think about stretching it out and flattening it, like you're paving a runway for incoming dick. Once you start sliding him deeper, you'll feel him reach the back of your throat. This is where most bitches tap out. But to go further, you need to:

Keep the tongue flat.

Stay relaxed.

Breathe through your nose.

Tilt your head back slightly to line up your throat and mouth.

Eventually, you'll find a "sweet spot" where everything lines up and he starts to slide in easier. That doesn't mean it won't feel intense. It will. But you'll be able to control it.

A Very Sticky Situation.
Want to train your technique without pressure? Try the Honey Challenge.

Coat his cock in something sticky: honey, syrup, chocolate sauce (I prefer dark), anything thick. Make it your mission to lick him clean.

No rushing. No jack-in-the-box bobbing. Just slow, deliberate, sticky-sweet attention. You'll discover pressure points, angles, rhythm, while getting him so worked up he might blow his load before you even get to deepthroating. Wouldn't that be marvelous?

Dick at Your Own Risk.
Even if you get it all the way down, don't ignore the signs. I shouldn't have to say the next part because it's painfully obvious, but a friend of a friend's cousin (who barely passed the bar) warned me about liability. True story. And since lawyers scare the ever-loving shit out of me (right behind clowns), I threw in the requisite legal warning in case some dipshit chick dies deepthroating a dildo:

Trouble breathing? Back off.

Feels too intense? Ease up, then go again.

Gagging hard? Stop and reset.

Puking on his dick will ruin your brand image. (Yeah, I said it.)

Or... just say, "Fuck it," deepthroating is overrated.

This isn't about powering through. It's about mastery over time. Once you learn to control the tongue, the breath, the angle, and the pressure, it turns into something filthy, smooth, and weirdly impressive. Like patting your head while rubbing his dick.

Final Thought.
Guys... before you start begging for this major blowjob upgrade:

Do you really want her to go through all this?

Unless she's into it, that "regular" blowjob is looking pretty fucking amazing right about now, isn't it?

And after I dropped this deepthroat manifesto on my site, my inbox exploded. I published one of the hottest replies on the next page.

... feedback from the deep

*You wanna know how
deepthroating feels? Ask the dick.
I can give you tips, but nothing
hits like hearing it from someone
who nearly blacked out from
pleasure.* — TechChick

After I dropped the deepthroating how-to on my site, my inbox went wild. Most people thanked me. Some admitted they'd never even tried. But one guy wrote in with a response so vivid, I needed a cigarette immediately afterward. I mentioned earlier that I thought deepthroating might be a little overrated.

He disagreed. Violently.

And I loved every word of it.

Here's what he wrote:
"First off, if it's not something she wants, it's not much fun for me. Sex needs two people into it, not one trying and one tolerating. I can't agree that it's overrated... maybe underrated.

The only 'problem' with getting full, all-the-way, deep head is the sensations are so strong I can't always keep up. I don't know who did who or what just happened, but it was sexy as fuck.

When a woman just nibbles, or takes in an inch or two, it's awkward. The rest of me is hanging out, untouched, unsexified, just there. But when she takes me all the way into her, I get slammed with waves of heat.

First there's the soft touch, lips, tongue, breath, unpredictable. Then I feel the back of her throat at the same time as her mouth, and that smooth, continuous slide that tells me this isn't play anymore. This is sex. She's not teasing. She's consuming.

At that point I don't know who's in control. I'm stuffing her throat; she's spinning me by my dick like a leash with me on it.

And here's the real win: it gives her an excuse to use her hands on me when I'm offering face time, so I don't have to ask. Overrated? Not even close."

— Love & good sex, Lou

TC comments: Well, holy shit and fuck me sideways.

When I first read this, all I could think was:
"Goddamn, I love my readers."

Lou, when you put it like that?
You're right.
Not overrated at all.

Thanks for turning me on *with my own fucking content.*

... the facial finale

Facials: hot in porn, risky in real life. Ask first, cowboy. — TechChick

When it comes to sex, some guys want to try everything at least once. Anal? Sure. Threesomes? Maybe. But one of the most awkwardly requested bucket list items?

The facial.

You've seen it in porn: a guy pulls out and paints her like a Jackson Pollock. Face, tits, stomach, wherever. Dramatic, visual, and sticky as hell. For a lot of guys, the fantasy of doing it in real life is intense.

After dozens of requests from guys asking how to ask for it without sounding like a psycho, I picked one of the better ones:

> **Dear TechChick,**
>
> I'm actually one of the lucky few who have no problem getting my girl to give me blowjobs but what I really want is to shoot my cum all over that pretty face of hers.
>
> Honestly, I don't even know how to ask. Do I say, "Hey, next time I'm about to cum, how about I pull out and shoot it in your eye?" I don't think she'll go for it, and I kinda feel like an asshole just bringing it up. Any advice?
>
> Don't worry, I'm not taking it that seriously. It's not like I'm one of those poor bastards who can't even get a blowjob.
> **— Squirter**

Dear Squirter,

Let's start here:

No, don't ask to shoot it in her eye.

Unless you're dating a pirate kink queen with cum-proof contact lenses, that's not the move.

Instead?

Just ask. Directly. Calmly. While she's giving you head, or after a hot session, say something like: "Can I cum on your face sometime? That really turns me on."

Say it like a gift you're hoping for, not a demand. Let her know it's about desire, not dominance.

And if she says yes? Two rules: Avoid the eyes and hair. Trust me. Make the cleanup part hot.

Wipe it off her with your fingers. Then take all that warm, wet cum and smear it between her legs. Rub it along her inner thighs. Get her soaked with it. Finger her until she's twitching. Rub her clit while you whisper how fucking turned on you are.

Make her cum with your cum.

By the time she's done panting, the facial won't be a mess to clean up. It'll be foreplay for round two.

If she says no? Respect that shit. No guilt, no "accidental slips," no weird groans or fake cramps just to pull out and launch your cum like a heat-seeking missile aimed at her forehead. Be the guy who asked and didn't get weird about it.

That's how you earn a maybe next time.

— **TechChick**

... juggling balls

Balls: underloved, overreactive, and surprisingly high-maintenance. Like toddlers, but hairier. — TechChick

Let's be real: balls don't get the respect they deserve. They're the unsung heroes of the penis party, always hanging around, taking hits, and shriveling to the size of peanuts if you even say "balls" out loud.

They don't get the same attention as cocks or clits. They're the roadies. The sidekicks. The emotional support animals of male anatomy.

But ignore the goofy little darlings completely? That's a missed opportunity.

Ball Basics

They're delicate, temperature-sensitive little fuckers. Basically, they're the drama queens of the dick region.

Most guys love having them handled, gently tugged, squeezed, licked. Others flinch if you so much as breathe on them the wrong way. So the rule is simple: start light and gauge the vibe.

Use your tongue. Use your hands. Use your breath. Cup them. Roll them. Stroke underneath.

The perineum, that's the patch of skin between the balls and the butthole (aka the "taint" or "gooch"). "It's the 'oh damn, where did that come from?' zone."

Just don't manhandle them like stress balls unless you've got a thing for high-pitched squealing and broken trust.

For the overachievers: Do all the above while sucking him off.

One hand on his shaft, one hand cradling the jewels, your mouth doing unspeakable things, and boom: he's in sensory overload.

If he's into edging, teasing the balls while backing off the shaft will drive him insane. If he's close, a little pressure and cupping during orgasm makes it even more intense.

Don't:

Yank.

Smack.

Treat them like a fidget toy.

Say their name out loud.

Bad Ball Jokes Because You Know I Can't Resist

What did one ball say to the other during sex?
Hang tight, bro. We're going in.

Why are testicles great at teamwork?
They've been hanging together forever!

Why did the testicles fail out of college?
They couldn't handle the pressure.

What's a testicle's favorite genre of music?
Soft rock.

Random Ball Facts

Testicles can double in size when a guy is really turned on. (No, you're not imagining it. They do get bigger before the grand finale. If only it worked that way with boobs.)

The word "testicle" comes from the Latin for witness. Apparently, Roman men used to swear oaths by grabbing their balls in court. Now that's commitment.

They crank out 200 million sperm a day. That's a lot of potential child support.

Final Thought...
You don't have to juggle balls like a circus pro. Just don't ignore them like socks in the dryer, tossed around and always left behind. A little

attention goes a long way. And if you ever get lost, just remember: when in doubt, ask.

Every guy has his own "ball settings," and the only way to get it right is to listen (and maybe watch his face for that "oh shit, too much!" expression).

Now go forth and juggle. Or fondle. Or just give 'em a gentle pat and a wink. Whatever you do, don't leave the little darlings hanging.

... dick size & bee stings

> Size may not matter, but bees
> definitely do. — TechChick

Small dick anxiety is real. And unfortunately, so is the internet, where every porn star is packing a Pringles can and every forum thread is filled with guys claiming they're 9.5 inches "on a bad day."

I once got a letter from a guy named Ralphy. He was convinced his dick was too small. He told me it was *5.5 inches long* and *8.5 inches around*.

Wait, what?
That's basically the girth of a Coke can. I grabbed one to check. Yup, terrifying. Ralphy, you're not small. You're armed.

But he was still hoping for more length, ideally 7 inches. He wanted to know if there was a free way to get there. So I gave him the honest answer:

"Uhhh, I don't know of any enlargement methods or products that really work. If they're out there, I doubt they're free. Hang in there, slugger."

What happened next was one of the weirdest mailbags I've ever gotten. Readers flooded me with suggestions on how to make your dick longer, thicker, stronger, and in some cases, *murdered by bees.*

Actual Responses From My Actual Readers:

"Stretch your dick for 20 minutes and milk it for another 30, five days a week. You'll see an inch in three months, two to three inches in a year. But most guys give up." — *Female reader*

TC Comment: So it's CrossFit for your cock?

"If you hold your dick shut while you blow your load, it might enlarge it. Maybe." — *Male reader*

TC Comment: Or maybe it explodes. Worth a shot?

"Gas a bee so it doesn't fly away. Then place it on your penis and make it sting you. It swells. Wear a cock ring to keep the swelling localized." — *Female reader*

TC Comment: I officially deny any legal responsibility for this jackass stunt. If you die from penis bee venom, that's on you.

"Don't forget the pump. Stick it in and pump it like hell. Claims to make it longer. Sounds safer than the bee thing." — *Same female reader just above (I shit you not)*

TC Comment: She's the Consumer Reports of DIY dick hacks, and honestly? I respect it."

"If you jerk off four times a week and whistle while you cum, your dick will get bigger. Something about muscle activation." — *Male reader*

TC Comment: Wasn't it Dopey who whistled while he worked? Full circle.

One guy even sent me a full technique manual. It was like penis yoga. Grasp. Pull. Shake. Lube. Repeat. Don't get too hard. Don't squeeze too tight. Don't forget to shake it off between sets. Honestly, I lost track around "pull toward the floor for 60 seconds."

TC Final Comment: Guys. We women have to spend five grand for a boob job. You're over here wrestling your dick like it's an unpaid intern. There's no guaranteed way to make your dick bigger. There are, however, about a dozen ways to injure yourself in the process.

And if you're genuinely smaller than average? That's not the end of your sex life; it's just the beginning of your skillset. Focus on mastering the art of fingers, tongue, and rhythm. Learn how to fuck with your whole body, not just your dick. Because a small cock with great technique will always be better than a big one attached to a lazy asshole.

Now step away from the bees.

... Q&A: Penis Puzzles

I wish women had a body part we were in love with the way men are in love with their own penises. Guys absolutely love their dicks. They talk to them, they play with them, they take care of them, they adore them. Their dick is the center of the universe. Women don't understand this in the slightest... and therein lies the problem.

Q. I know you already talked about dick size earlier, but I still feel like I'm too small. Even if I'm technically 'average,' I can't stop comparing myself to porn stars or online forums where everyone's swinging a third leg. Am I ever going to stop feeling inadequate?

A. I get this so often I could write an entire book just on Small Dick Anxiety. Yes, we covered this in "dick size & bee stings," but it's worth repeating: average is not small. And even if you're smaller than average, you can still be a rockstar in bed. Women care way more about how you use it than how many inches you're packing. So instead of spiraling down the comparison rabbit hole, work on your rhythm, touch, and presence. Technique beats size. Every. Single. Time. You are more than enough, unless you're out here playing with bees again. Then maybe ice it.

Q. I have foreskin. Do most women prefer cut or uncut guys? Should I be worried about it?

A. Here's the truth: Some women have a preference, but most don't care as long as you're clean, confident, and know how to use what you've got. In the U.S. and Canada, more women say they like circumcised, but plenty love uncut once they've tried it. Foreskin can make sex smoother and sometimes more fun. Bottom line: It's not a dealbreaker for most women, and if it is for her, she probably doesn't belong in your bed anyway. Take care of your dick, rock what you've got, and focus on being a good lover, not on the "wardrobe."

Q. My dick curves to the left when it's hard, and I get a little clear fluid at the tip when I'm turned on. Is that normal?

A. Not only is it normal, it's practically expected. Most dicks curve a little when hard. Left, right, up... hell, some guys could open beer bottles with that upward arc. It's just how your ligaments and blood flow work. Unless it hurts, interferes with sex, or looks like a boomerang in flight, don't sweat it. Some partners actually love it because it hits different spots. So don't think "weird." Think "angle of attack." As for the clear fluid, that's just pre-cum. It means you're turned on. The body's way of prepping the runway. Perfectly normal. If anything, congrats: it makes great lube.

Q. Sometimes my dick gets hard randomly even when I'm not turned on. What's the deal? **A.** The deal is: you're alive and male. Random boners happen. On average, a dozen times a day, yes, even while you're asleep. (That's what I call dream logic.) Think of it like a system check: your body doing a surprise fire drill in your pants. You could be eating cereal or watching Jeopardy, and boom, dick's up. Totally normal. Totally annoying if you're in public wearing sweatpants.   Wait, you don't wear sweatpants in public, do you?

... A Day in the Life: Of Dick

You think writing a chapter about dicks is all porn stars, wild confessions, and inboxes full of gratitude?

Please.

Here's what a real day in the life looks like behind the scenes at Sex Bytes HQ:

Wake up to three new emails titled "Am I too small?" and one from a guy who attached a photo of his dick next to a stapler for scale. (Dude: Use a ruler. Or, you know, don't send me your dick at breakfast.)

Field a message from a 19-year-old demanding to know if his left nut is "supposed to hang lower" or if he's "broken for life." (**TC's Reply:**

"You're fine. Tell your mom to stop reading your browser history, then walk away knowing that lefty just likes to stretch his legs first.")

Spend an hour deleting spam for penis pills, pumps, and "guaranteed" enlargement creams. (If any of them worked, I'd be writing this from a goddamn private island.)

Moderate a comment thread that's devolved into a heated, deeply weird debate about foreskin, featuring two Americans, a Brit, and a guy from New Zealand who claims he can tie his in a knot. (I did a little mouth puke visualizing this. Then I swallowed, god help me.)

Write a reply to a woman who wants to know if it's "normal" that her boyfriend named his dick "The Situation." (It's not, but hey, at least he's creative.)

And somewhere in between the jokes and the chaos, I remember this: dick insecurity is real. It's cultural. It's generational. It's relentless.

I've answered hundreds—maybe thousands—of men. Kind ones. Scared ones. Angry ones. They've all built their entire self-worth around a few inches of flesh.
They're not looking for porn tips, or even sex advice. They're looking for reassurance they never got.
And sometimes I give it, even when I'm not sure they'll believe me.

Take a break to explain to my accountant once again why "ButtStuffBonanza" is a legitimate business expense. He says it doesn't "look right." I told him, "Since when have my finances ever looked right? And don't be so judgy."

Try to write a serious answer about premature ejaculation, only to get interrupted by my cat walking across the keyboard, last step on the larger "enter" key, and sending "asdfjklj" to 1200 subscribers. (Sorry, everyone.)

End the day with a bottle of wine (that's only four *official* glasses by the way), a stack of unanswered "Can you rate my dick?" emails, and the realization that no matter how many dicks you write about, there's always another one in the queue.

And that's just Wednesday.

But if it's ever quiet in Dickland, trust me, it means it's Jesus' second coming, there's no one left to write me, and men everywhere have finally mastered their dicks, and I'm out of a job. Ha. As if.

Put It In, Then What?

Yes, This Is the **Fucking** Chapter

... round one: feral, fast, & furniture-breaking

Positions are like outfits. You need a few that always work, one or two showstoppers, and something weird you only try when you're drunk. — TechChick

Round One is for when you want to fuck like you might break the furniture, or each other. It's the kind of sex you feel the next day, when something's sore and you're still grinning.

75

Positions: The Ones That Fuck Back You need a solid stack in your repertoire, and we're all out here scouting for new entries on the keeper side of the mental fucklist.

The classic triple threat (missionary, girl on top, doggy style) still slaps. They work. They're reliable. You could pull them off blindfolded, tied up, and half-asleep, and they'd still deliver.

But humans need variety. In life and in bed. Especially in bed. So we chase more. New angles. Better access. Nasty upgrades.

Here are a few worth adding to your fucklist.

But first: Doggy-Style

People on death row get a last meal. Doggy would be my death row last-fuck request.

There's a reason this one never goes out of style. It's animalistic, primal, and does a total mindfuck on both partners, exactly what you want when you're chasing that can't-wait-another-second energy.

I'm not including this because it's new (please, if you were one of the cool kids, you've been doing this since puberty). I'm including it because it always delivers.

If you're chasing the mythical G-spot: This is your best shot (if it exists, which it doesn't... but let's pretend). With her on all fours and you thrusting from behind, you've got the perfect angle to attack that elusive spot.

Want to level up? Reach around and rub her clit while you fuck. Or let your balls do the talking, slapping against her ass with every thrust just to remind you both you're alive.

Sometimes the classics are classics for a reason.

Doggy isn't a style, it's a staple. If you've got hang-ups about it, don't worry, keep reading. I've got entire sections to help shake off your kinky vanilla cringe.

The Wall Fuck

You're standing. She's standing. Her back hits the wall, and everything else disappears. This isn't a lazy man's fuck. It's fast and filthy, with just enough danger to make your blood roar. Her leg around your waist. Her arms around your neck. You've got to hold her up and hold your shit together, because she will fall if you don't. That's not a metaphor. She will literally collapse if you're not gripping her tight.

Now, let's talk wardrobe: short skirt, no panties. Loose blouse that slips off a shoulder when things get frantic. You pin her to the wall, hike the skirt, and slide in. You've got leverage. She's got friction burns on her shoulder blades. Nobody's complaining.

She's clinging. You're driving. It's messy, rushed, and goddamn perfect.

This is pure, unfiltered, primal sex—no thinking, just instinct. Me Tarzan, you Jane.

No one's worried about technique. Nobody's worried about anything except not falling and not stopping.

> **Wild Card: The Elevator** For when you want to take "up against the wall" literally. Lift her up, pin her to the wall, and thrust upward. Gravity-defying, adrenaline-pumping, and guaranteed to test your core strength.

Only attempt if you trust your grip and she doesn't mind drywall burns.

And when it's over?

Don't walk away like some douchebag. Drop to your knees, keep her pinned, and finish what you started with your mouth. Let her ride the aftershocks while you get soaked. Just don't forget: gravity's still a thing. So is aftercare.

Bent-Over Standing

There's a reason this one gets cast in 9 out of 10 porn scenes. It's fast, rough, and filthy as hell when done right. She bends forward, hands on the wall, a desk, the obligatory car hood, wherever, and you enter from behind. Standing. No frills, no prep speech. Just raw, ragged breathing and the kind of angle that makes both of you cuss like sailors mid-thrust.

This is doggy's evil stepsister. Less "sexy arch," more "shove her skirt up and fuck." You're upright, so you've got full control: hips, shoulders, hair, whatever. And if she drops her chest and locks her legs? Game over. That's porn physics. With handprints.

No bullshit tip: If you're taller, use a step-stool or have her tilt her pelvis up. Porn makes it look easy-breezy, but real life needs props.

Wild Card: The Standing Spin Ready to get acrobatic? She plants her hands on the floor. You grab her legs and lift. Now you're behind, holding her up and thrusting like a maniac in a gym class gone wild. It's a workout. It's a spectacle. And if you both survive, bragging rights for life. The real prize: Deep-as-deep-can-go penetration. Downside: She may need a helmet in case you launch her into a dresser.

The Sit/Stand

Countertop. Table. Washer. Anything sturdy enough to hold her weight and your enthusiasm. She's sitting on the edge, legs spread, ass barely hanging on. You're standing between her thighs, lining up like you're about to fuck the logic out of her. Knock that piece of crap blender off the counter.

This one's all about depth. When she wraps her legs around your waist or throws them up onto your shoulders if she's extra bendy, you can go so deep it almost rewires her. And you? You're not lasting long. Something about standing while she's wide open like a buffet with your name on it... it shortens the fuse. Don't fight it. Fast can be fantastic.

Want to slow it down? Grab her hips and take control. Ease out 'til you're barely inside, then push back in like you mean it. Kiss her. Watch her. Make sure she feels every inch in her spine.

Fair warning: most kitchen furniture wasn't built for thrust impact.

> **Wild Card: The Kitchen Sink** Sex isn't just for beds and tables and counters and floors and chairs and the top of dog crates. Try propping her up on the kitchen sink, legs wrapped around you, warm water running. It's spontaneous, messy, and might end with a minor flood. Check this out: If you've got one of those spray-nozzle thingies on the faucet and want her to cum in 60 seconds flat, aim it right between her thighs and fuck her clit with it. It's motherfucking heaven. And I'm an atheist (I think... I'm still exploring shit.)

The Reverse Rider

You're in a chair. Not some rickety-ass kitchen stool, but something military-grade solid. Legs planted. Back supported. Cock ready.

She climbs on, but not to face you. She turns around, lowers herself onto your lap, and suddenly your view is all curve, bounce, and filthy bliss. Her back is to you. Her body on full display. And you're just... watching. Guiding. Gripping her hips like you're steering a dream.

She's braced on the arms of the chair, riding like she's squatting on your dick at the gym. But the longer it lasts, the weaker her knees get. That's when you step in: hands on her hips, helping her move. Slow. Deep. Fucking relentless.

Want to level up? Right before you cum, lift her just enough to unload all over her ass. Watch it. Feel it. Commit that shit to memory.

This one's for when you want to fuck her like a fantasy and leave her too wrecked to walk straight.

Wild Card: The Spinning Top In porn, a "spinner" is a petite girl who's light enough to flip, toss, or spin into damn near any position. But in this version, she's on top, facing away, and grinding in slow circles. Her hips are doing all the work, rotating over your cock with a rhythm that is, well... indescribable.

Then she pivots. Shifts. Maybe spins around to face you. Maybe not. She's in full control, and your job is to just hang the hell on.

This one's all about movement. Not bouncing, but rotating. Not pounding, but riding. And if she wants to get creative and do a full 180 on you mid-thrust? Salute that shit. Just don't expect her to whirl like a literal top unless you've got a camera crew and a suspension rig. Here's where it gets fun: Works best on a swivel chair. Or an unmade bed. Or anywhere she can show off and you can shut up.

Masturbation break. Hydrate, then return for Round Two.

... round two: hey! there's a person attached

Round One gets you off. Round Two fucks you up a little. If Round One is a quickie in a stairwell, Round Two is the fuck you think about later.

Positions: The Ones That Stay With You
After the frenzy comes the connection. These positions slow things down without softening the edge, bringing deeper rhythm, full-body contact, and mutual payoff.
Less porn loop, more "get in my head."
Still intense. Just hits different.

The Butterfly
Bed, table, counter. It doesn't matter, as long as you've got height on her. You're standing. She's lying back. Legs up, knees bent, feet resting on your shoulders like you're about to push her into another dimension. Slide a pillow under her ass to tilt her pelvis just right. You want that angle. You need that angle. One hand under each hip to lift her just enough, and now you're right where you need to be. No wasted motion. All payoff.

This is G-spot central (doesn't exist). Deep thrusts hit different here, especially if she's got her hands free to rub her clit while you hold her steady and drive it home. The position practically begs for slow, intentional movement, none of that jackhammer nonsense.

Think sensual wrecking ball. It's intimate without being soft. Physical without being frantic. And if you're doing it right? She'll finish with her thighs shaking and a face that says, "damn right, I came."

> **Wild Card: The Winged Victory** Start in butterfly position. She's on her back, legs up, feet on your shoulders. But here's the twist:

grab her ankles and push her legs all the way back, folding her nearly in half.

Think contortionist meets cock worship.

Now her pelvis is practically vertical, hips tilted to give you absurdly deep access. Her ass is hovering. Her moans are pure, primal punctuation.

Here's the power move: With her legs pressed back and your chest over hers, you've got max control and eye contact. It's part dominance, part stretch session, and all sensation.

Warning: Don't attempt if she's got tight hamstrings or a chiropractor on speed dial.

The Chair Grind

Pick a chair. Not a barstool, not a duct-taped beanbag from the basement. Something sturdy, stable, and ready to hold the weight of a damn good time. You sit down. She straddles you, facing forward, knees bent, feet planted.

This one's not about bouncing. It's about grinding. She leans in, chest to chest, lips to neck, and starts moving slow. Tiny circles. Subtle shifts. Her clit pressed tight against your pubic bone. It's friction over thrust, rhythm over speed. A full-body pulse.

Your hands are free. Use them. Back, hips, hair, tits, whatever's calling to you. Pull her closer. Let her ride the pressure wave until she shudders, pants, and clutches your shoulders like a lifeline.

This is the position where eye contact turns into eye fucks. Where breathing syncs. Where everything else fades out.

Wild Card: The Rocking Chair Yes, really. Sit her in a rocking chair and climb on. Let the motion do some of the work while your hands and mouths handle the rest. It's playful, offbeat, and surprisingly hot. Rocking chairs are making a comeback, and this is one hell of a reason why.

The Clock

It sounds complicated, but stay with me. This one sneaks up on you, then wrecks you in the best way.

She's on her back. You're on your side, facing her. Let's say her left side. Now picture a clock: your head is at 12:00, hers is at 2:00. You're forming an L-shape. It's not geometry. It's geometry that fucks back.

From here, two killer options:
Option one: She raises both legs and drapes them over your thigh, scooting her ass close so you can slide in from the side.
Option two: She pulls one knee toward her chest and lets the other leg hang over your thigh. It's a subtle twist, literally, and it creates a whole new kind of pressure and depth.

This angle gives you incredible friction, deeper strokes, and full access to her body. You can kiss her. Watch her. Finger her while you're inside. It's connected, off-center, and unexpectedly intense.
You've probably done this one a hundred times, just not like this.

> **Wild Card: The Sundial** Think of this as the Clock... but mobile. Start in the position above, then slowly rotate, her legs shifting, your angle changing. Try moving from 2:00 to 4:00 to 6:00, adjusting pressure and position with each shift. Every tick delivers a new sensation. It's slow, experimental, and sexy as hell. Finally, a use for math that ends in an orgasm.

Spooning

It looks sweet. It is. But don't get it twisted, this isn't just cuddling with benefits. This is a whole-body connection, disguised as laziness.

You're both lying on your sides, you behind her. One arm under her head or around her waist. One hand free to roam. You slide in from behind, hips in sync, bodies flush. Everything's connected, like two dirty spoons in a perfect little spoon world.

This is the position for sleepy morning sex.

For when it's too late, too early, or just too good to stop. You're both half-awake but fully locked in. You can fuck, nap, and dirty talk all in the same breath, and never once leave the sheets.

Don't underestimate the power here. Spooning lets you fuck with feeling. The thrusts are slower. Deeper. More deliberate. And if she reaches behind to grab your ass and pull you in tighter? Yeah. That's the move.

> **Wild Card: The Lazy Lock** Too tired to flip? Stay spooned, but throw her top leg up and over your hip for better access and angle. It's the ultimate "just one more round" trick. Zero effort, all reward. Great for hangovers, hotel naps, 420 highs, or any time you want to fuck without moving more than absolutely necessary.

The Bridge

This one's half sex position, half performance art. She lies on her back and pushes her hips up into a full bridge. Feet flat, knees bent, ass in the air like she's ready to be worshipped. You kneel between her legs and thrust upward into her. Deep. Direct. With intention.

It's not a long-term strategy. Her thighs will burn, and your knees might start complaining, but the payoff is stupidly good. You get full visibility, deep thrust access, and a tight squeeze from every angle. Her core is engaged. Her breath is a mess. And you're the reason.

Here's the hack: This position turns into a whole-ass workout if she holds it long enough. Or, for a sexier cheat, slide a firm pillow under her lower back and let her hips rest on it. You still get the angle. She still gets that "what planet am I on?" energy.

> **Wild Card: The Suspension Bridge** Take the bridge and go full acrobat. She holds her hips up while you hook her thighs over your shoulders and stand. Yes, stand. Then bend forward and lift her off the bed slightly. Now she's weightless, you're in charge, and the whole thing feels like Cirque du So-Lay-You-Down. Proceed only if you trust your balance, your quads, and your flaky chiropractor.

Masturbation break. (You're welcome.)

... the finger fuck

There is just something about fingerfucking that is deliciously nasty and erotic. Done in the way in which I'm about to describe, that is.

The thing about fingerfucking is it is just so specific and methodical in its purpose. The view and feel are incredible. And her knowing you are watching and looking at her sooo close is beyond words!

She has to be very comfortable and secure with herself and trusting of you, more so even than with fucking or eating her out, probably. Because if you do this in the way I describe... my god... you will see EVERYTHING and learn more about her in one session than you can possibly imagine.

She's going to realize this very soon into it, so hopefully that comfort level, security, and trust already exist. She needs to be totally uninhibited because not only are you going to send her through the roof, you're going to know damn near everything about her by the time you finish!

Position:
Preferably her in a very nice, cushy, overstuffed chair... one she can lean back into and feel sooo relaxed! Candles lit! Yes! Absolutely! Lots of them, though... you need to be able to see everything... soft light... OK? Pre-plan here... No noise, except something very soft in the background... no television... have it together! High preference for her in lingerie... loose lingerie, something soft and flowing... alright, you will be kneeling on the floor in front of her... facing her... watching her lovely face to start.

Getting There:
Begin with soft, gentle kisses on the mouth, neck, and ears… whispers… slooowly… sweetly… take your time. Enjoy her… everything very slow… get into her… make her warm… relax her… gentle, loving, slow, soft kisses… love licks… nibbling… move down… breasts… nipples… moan… lots of time here… soft sucking… now back up again… all over again… sooo slowly… teasing… loving… OK, back down… breasts and nipples… all over again… now, we move down… stomach… pubic area… but not there… not yet… just all around there… now, thighs… softly… no tickling though… keep it together… spend a lot of time here… everything nice and slow… watch her… and when it's time… move to her pussy…

Sending Her:
…begin moving your fingers all around the outside of her pussy… slooowly… not inside of her… all around her… if she is not soaking wet, you did not do the above worth a damn… OK, just nice and easy… slip inside of her… watch her… this is the best part… watch her… very easy… very gently… very slowly… out… and… in… slowly, now… keep this going… your other hand is caressing her body… your mouth is bent down kissing her… not her clit… not yet… slowly

finger-fuck her… keep everything else going… now… another finger… do it all over again… she should be gripping… if she's not… ask her to… whisper it… watch her… watch her… watch her… look at her spread legs… her pussy so close… your fingers slipping slowly… inside… and out… everything creamy and warm… juices dripping… play with her nipples… keep caressing… now… lick her clit… keep the slow finger-fucking going… not fast… slow… tease… prolong… kiss and suck… her clit… other hand… still exploring her… eat her pussy while fingers are fucking her… caressing with other hand… max out her senses… max out her senses… max out her senses… lots going on… she doesn't know which way is up… now… if she's into anal… take her hot, sticky pussy juice… and go there… still eating her out… still finger-fucking… all at once… very intense… you're in control… moaning… eat her pussy the best you know how… and bring her there… all the way… send her shaking… bring her to orgasm… feel her pussy grip your fingers as she cums… nice feeling… for her… and you…

OK now… come down easy with her… nothing abrupt… go with her reaction… bring her back to earth slowly… gently… let her absorb what just happened to her… keep loving her… just caress her… and smile at her…

…damn. That's how you do it.

… the titty fuck

The titty-fucking image is right up there with the cumshot as the porntastic visual jackpot. Guys love to see a dick, especially their own, sandwiched between a pair of big, bouncing tits. Doesn't matter what the girl looks like. She just needs to have big ol' knockers.

To achieve it, a man only needs two things: big ol' titties and a willing girl attached to them. The titty fuck does not work with small tits, no matter how hot she is. You need ample mammary flesh, no getting around it.

Lube the girls' tits up with something super slippery, like baby oil, and rub it all over your dick too. Now, mess around with a few positions to get it just right, and when you do, the girl should wrap her tits around your dick and squeeze them together from the outside, holding you in place.

Have her start moving them in an up-and-down motion at the same time she's squeezing. If she's the coordinated type (she's got big tits, so I doubt it), have her move one tit up while she moves the other down and keep this motion going non-stop. Are you visualizing this? Her tits are fucking your dick more so than the other way around.

The baby oil will get very nice and warm and will feel divine. Once you are pumping away and the two of you have your rhythm, she can't make the mistake of working too fast or too furiously. You'll probably cum quick once the team effect kicks in, giving you the ultimate visual jackpot: the cumshot AND the tittyfuckshot, all in one glorious mess.

Let's be honest: titty-fucking is the sex equivalent of fireworks, loud, messy, and mostly for the people watching. If you've got the right equipment (big tits, a willing partner, and a bottle of baby oil), go for it. Just remember, this one's all about the visuals and the ego trip. Nobody's getting off from the friction alone. But if you both love the show? Enjoy the jackpot, cumshot and tittyfuckshot, all in one. Sometimes, sex is just about the spectacle.

... performance, fast ejac

Think too much about performance and it's freak-out time for a lot of guys. If there's a performance problem and you're under 30, it's usually premature ejaculation. Big annoyance, but there are some little things you can do to make that wonderful cock of yours hang in there a little longer

Frequency:
The more often you have orgasms, the longer you'll last during intercourse. Translation: have sex more often, and your endurance goes up. You know this already, right? Go three weeks without getting laid, and you're a goner in five minutes. But if you're having sex five to seven times a week, by day five you're up to 20 minutes before you blow.

Distraction:
Another trick, if you can pull it off, is to get sex off the brain while you're having it. Think about the Braves choking in the postseason, or what the 80-year-old neighbor looks like naked. Not super practical, but hey, if it works, it works.

Pre-Jackoff:
Go to the bathroom and jack off like a furious little pimply-faced teen right before sex. This one actually works. Everyone knows the second round lasts longer.

Condoms:
Wear one and slow yourself down. Yes, condoms suck, but if you're serious about lasting longer, they help. Thicker condoms dull sensation at the tip, but don't kill the pleasure. Still, nothing beats bare cock on skin... sorry, got distracted for a sec.

Creams:

Desensitizing creams can help, but be careful. The good ones help you last. The bad ones freeze your dick to the point of numbness (or so I've heard). Test before you go all in. And for god's sake, don't ask for head unless you want her lips numb and her mouth useless for the rest of the night.

Practice-Practice:

Masturbating, that is. But don't just jerk off to finish; try stopping yourself once or twice and then starting again. Stop right when you're about to cum, wait for the urge to pass, then go again. Do this a few times a week and you'll build real-world stamina.

Here's the deal: This "start-stop" technique, also called edging, is a proven way to build control and last longer, both solo and with a partner. The idea is to bring yourself close to orgasm, pause, let the urge fade, and then start again. It's a little frustrating at first, but the payoff is real.

Pulling Out:

This is probably the most common in-the-moment move. Most guys know when they're about to blow, so if you can master a little self-control and pull out right before, you can last longer. Let your partner know what you're doing. She'll get it. Do this a few times in one session, and your final orgasm will hit harder.

Final note:

How long you last isn't a dealbreaker for most women. What matters is that you take care of her first. Spend time on foreplay, get her off before intercourse, and she won't care if you finish fast. Throw in some dirty talk, like 'I can't help it, you drive me wild, I can't wait, I'm gonna cum...' Flip the script and blame her for being too damn hot. Mischievous, but highly effective.

Final-final note:
If you want to get nerdy about it, look up the 'stop-start' or 'squeeze' technique, or even try Kegels. Yeah, guys can do them too. Just maybe don't brag about your pelvic floor routine to your gym bros.

And then there are guys like this, who it's really difficult to feel sorry for:

Q. I am a 25-year-old male that has been in many, many, many relationships with very attractive women. All my life I have not been able to perform a "quickie," "nooner," etc.... It normally takes me 1 1/2 to 2 hours to cum... I have stopped masturbating, but that has only cut down about 15 minutes. When I cum it is comparable to Peter North's load... (**TC comment:** Peter North is a famous porn star known for his ability to shoot gigantic loads.) I don't have a problem pleasing my girlfriend, but if it is 10 or 11 p.m. and she wants it, then I get the short end of the deal... Can you help me cum faster....

A. Boo hoo. Man, you've got it tough. Honestly, you sound like a dream come true. :-) Ok, one suggestion for you is to try to get yourself very worked up before you begin having sex. You can do this by really letting yourself go with a favorite fantasy, looking at porn, etc.

Another idea: if you know you want to go for the quickie, masturbate almost to the point of cumming just before having sex with your girlfriend. Then engage in a little foreplay and go straight to intercourse. You should be more than ready to get off quickly. Now it's her turn. Don't forget to take care of her. You got your quickie, and she's happy too.

... hard to get hard

The flip side of cumming too fast? Not getting hard at all. Hey, you preemie jackers, quit your bitching. It could be worse... It could be worse... you could be scrolling back up, whispering "please work" under your breath.

Q. Sometimes I lose my erection halfway through sex. Is this a sign something's wrong?

A. Not necessarily. Sometimes your brain's not in the game, sometimes your body's just not feeling it, and sometimes you've had three too many vodka sodas. Penises are moody little bastards. If it happens every now and then, don't panic. If it's happening a lot, talk to a doctor; could be physical, could be stress, or maybe your dick is just saying, "You jerked me off three times today; give me a fucking break."

Either way, don't be a dick to your partner just because your ego took a hit. Women don't care that you lost it; we care if you act weird about it and then disappear. Stay cool, stay present, and remember: the night's not over just because your dick took a break mid-fuck.

Real talk: Erectile dysfunction (ED, impotence, whatever you want to call it) is a real thing for millions of guys, young and old. It's frustrating as hell, and it can feel like your body's betraying you. But it's fixable. If you're not dealing with major mental or emotional stuff (let's face it, who the fuck isn't!), odds are it's physical and there are solutions.

have one word for you: VIAGRA. It works. So do a bunch of other meds. If you're struggling, talk to a doctor and get some help; don't just suffer in silence or pretend it's not happening.

If all else fails, just remember: nobody ever got dumped for being too good at oral. Now get back in there and make some magic, dick or no dick.

... her tight backdoor

Let's talk about the forbidden zone: the anus. For straight folks, it's the taboo hole; guys want in, and women usually want a "keep the fuck out" sign. Why? Because pain is a real possibility, and so is a mental freak-out.

Let's be honest: half the reason so many guys want to try anal is because it's "forbidden fruit." Taboo is catnip for the human brain. If society says "don't," you want to. For some, that's the whole thrill. For others, it's a shame spiral waiting to happen. Either way, the "we're not supposed to do this" energy is real, and it's why you need to talk about it, not just try to sneak it in and hope for the best.

If you're both genuinely curious (not just following some porn script), the taboo can make it hotter. But if you're just doing it because you think you "should," or you're scared to even say the word "anal" out loud, you're not ready. Talk about it. Laugh about it. Own the weirdness. Then, if you both want to, get on with the lube and the fun.

If you're the fuck-er, you've got two obstacles: first, the taboo itself (it's a mindfuck); second, her fear of pain (which is legit). The only way through both? Communication, patience, and a metric ton of lube.

If you're the fuck-ee, you've got two obstacles: first, pain; second, pain. The only way through both? Same answer—communication, patience, and a metric ton of lube.

Prep: Cleanliness & Comfort

If you want anal to be hot and not a horror flick, prep is your friend. Lube, patience, and a little planning—trust me, it's worth it. The anus is a butt; it's designed for exit, not entrance. If you don't clear it out, you might end up with shit on your dick, her, the sheets... maybe all three. Embarrassing? Yep. Fixable? Also yep.

How to Keep it (Mostly) Mess-Free

Go to the bathroom first. Empty your bowels and give it a little time (20–30 minutes) before play.

Hop in the shower and wash up. Use warm water (not hot), and just clean the outside and a little inside with a finger; no need to go deep.

If you want to be extra sure, a small bulb syringe with lukewarm water (not soap, not hot, not a giant enema) can help, but don't overdo it. One or two gentle rinses is enough. Too much can irritate or dehydrate the colon.

Skip heavy or greasy foods that day. Trust me.

Lay down a towel, seriously, not just for "just in case." Make it a big, thick one you're not emotionally attached to.

If you're even a little worried, have wet wipes or a washcloth ready for cleanup. Or, if you skipped all the prep and decided to live dangerously, maybe grab five washcloths and a mop bucket. You've been warned.

If you do get a little mess? Don't freak out. It's normal. Laugh it off, clean up, and move on.

Mental Prep & Communication

Talk about it before you're naked. Boundaries, worries, safe words, and what to do if anyone wants to stop (hint: scream STOP)—get it all out in the open.

If she's nervous, encourage her to practice on herself first (fingers, small toys, etc.) so she knows what to expect.

Make sure she feels 100% in control. She can say stop at any time, and you'll listen.

Lube: Non-Negotiable

The OGs: K-Y Jelly and Astroglide, water-based, classic, and fine for backdoor adventures. If you want something thicker, Boy Butter is a cult favorite (but not condom-safe). These days, there are tons of specialty anal lubes, but if it's thick, slick, and body-safe, you're good to go. Silicone lubes are also great for anal: super slippery, long-lasting, and safe with condoms and toys (unless they're silicone toys).

Rule #1: Never go in dry. Ever.

Foreplay: The Real Key

If she's not soaking the sheets, don't even think about going near that hole.

Whisper in her ear, squeeze her nipples, keep her relaxed.

Start with a well-lubed finger—go slow. If she tenses up, back off.

When she's relaxed, maybe try a second finger or a small plug.

Once she's into it, lube up your cock (seriously, half a tube) and ease just the tip in. Go slow. Don't pull out. If you do, you're not getting back in. Dead serious.

Keep it slow and gentle. No jackhammering. No pile-driving. No "watch this, babe" bullshit. This isn't about performance. It's about her pleasure. Stimulate her nipples, use your fingers, add a vibe, and rub her clit.

If she's taking your whole cock in her ass, the least you can do is make sure she's shaking. Come quick, keep it cool, and there's a good chance she'll let you do it again.

Aftercare: TLC for Her
Clean up together: Shower off, use warm water, and be gentle; her skin is sensitive.

Praise her: She just did something vulnerable and intense. Tell her how hot and amazing she is.

Check in: Ask how she feels, if anything hurts, or if she needs anything.

Moisturize: If she's sore, a little unscented lotion or coconut oil around (not in) the area can help.

No ass-to-pussy: When you pull out, do NOT go near her pussy with that dick. Infection city. Don't do it.

Bottom line
Anal is all about trust, patience, prep, and lube. If you can't handle all four, stick to the front door. And if you make a mess? Welcome to the anal-sex club.

... his *tighter* backdoor

Answering a late-night DM from a guy who wants to know if it's "normal" that he wants his girlfriend to peg him. (Short answer: Yes. Long answer: Welcome to the future, my dude.)

Uhh, anal goes both ways.

Hey TC,

I really get turned on by the idea of my girlfriend sticking her finger in my ass during sex. Thing is, she never even goes near the area and I'm kind of embarrassed to come straight out and ask for it. Anyway, I know you get a lot of mail and was wondering if this is normal or not. Could I have gay tendencies because I fantasize about this?
Peace out, Rick

Hey Rick,

Yep, you're normal, don't worry about it. And even if it's not "normal," who gives a shit? I have no idea what normal is. The whole concept is way overrated. The real win is just getting your head in the right place so you feel okay about asking for what you want. Open communication is everything. I know it's easier said than done, but someone's gotta start somewhere.

One other thing: generally, people do to their partner what they want done to themselves, or what feels good to them on the receiving end.

For example, if a girl is always licking your ear, chances are she likes that done to her. If you don't want to come right out and talk to her about your anal curiosity, try playing with her ass a bit and see how she responds. If she seems into it, you're halfway to getting this reciprocated. If she freaks out when you even go near the area, odds are she's not going to be sticking anything in you anytime soon.

As for the "gay tendencies" part: you already know the answer. You said you like the idea of your girlfriend fingering your ass during sex, not the idea of a 350-pound hairy dude mounting you and ramming you with a nine-incher. Big difference.

Fact is, the anus is an erogenous zone for both sexes, so relax. If her dainty, tangerine-orange-polished finger feels good up your butthole, everything is "normal."

Peace out, TC

... yeah, I've faked it

This is a public service announcement for every woman who's ever faked it, is faking it, or is even thinking about faking it:

STOP. Just... stop.

Faking it is the absolute worst thing you can do for your sex life. Seriously, you're not sparing anyone's feelings; you're just signing yourself up for a lifetime of "meh" sex and a partner who thinks he's Casanova because you keep giving him a standing O for doing the bare minimum.

Every time you fake it, you're teaching him that whatever random thing he just did is the magic move. So guess what? He'll keep doing it. Again. And again. And again. Welcome to your own personal Groundhog Day of bad orgasms (aka: none at all).

Let's get real: faking it isn't just about avoiding an awkward moment. It's lying, straight up. You're lying to him, and you're lying to yourself. You're building a wall between you and any chance of actual, mind-blowing sex.

You're also setting yourself up for resentment, frustration, and a partner who will be completely blindsided when you finally snap and tell him the truth. And that's just fucking mean.

And if you're faking it because you want to "make him feel good" or you're too embarrassed to say what you want? That's not noble; it's self-sabotage. You deserve better. He deserves better. Your relationship deserves better.

If you keep faking, you're basically guaranteeing that you'll never get what you actually want in bed, because how the hell is he supposed to know what works if you're giving him a gold star for failure? And his "failure" is YOUR damn fault for not telling him and showing him what you want (major turn-on for him by the way).

And for the dudes out there still wondering, "How can I tell if she's faking it?" If she looks and sounds anything like Meg Ryan in When Harry Met Sally, she is. Sorry, bro.

Bottom line:
Faking it is a one-way ticket to a dead bedroom and a relationship built on bullshit. Want better sex? Get honest. Speak up. Stop giving out Oscars for performances you hate.

Good luck. And, I mean that. Simple show-and-tell will catapult you to the orgasmic life you righteously deserve.

... Q&A: Fucking Overload

Q: How long is sex supposed to last?

A: "Supposed to" is bullshit. Some people think if you're not jackhammering for an hour, you're failing. Reality check: the average romp is around 5 to 7 minutes of actual penetration (3 to 4 minutes if you have my shitty luck), and that's perfectly fine.

If you want a marathon, go run a race. If you want great sex, focus on quality, not your stopwatch. And for the record, most women care way more about what happens before and after than how long you can pump.

Q: How often should a couple have sex?

A: However often you both want to. Some couples are rabbits; some are hibernating bears. There's no magic number. If you're both happy, you're doing it right. If one of you isn't, talk about it before you end up as roommates with benefits (or just roommates), then ex-roommates.

Q: Does porn mess up real sex?

A: Only if you think porn is a documentary. Porn is fantasy: angles, edits, and Olympic-level flexibility. Don't use it as a playbook; use it for ideas (if you want), but remember: real sex is messier, funnier, and way more interesting than trying to imitate a pornstar. Because let's be real, even the weirdest dudes get laid in those movies. Real life is about connection, not casting.

Q: How do I make sex less awkward?

A: Laugh. Seriously. Sex is weird, bodies are weird, and something will go wrong eventually: a wet fart, a WTF cramp out of the blue, a weird noise that you're unsure of the orifice it came from and don't really care to. If you can laugh together, you're already having better sex than half the planet. Drop the "perfect" act and just enjoy the ride.

... A Day in the Life: Fucking

People think running an adult site is some endless orgy of pleasure. Like I'm just lounging around in silk sheets, fielding fan mail from grateful couples, and taking breaks to test out the latest sex toy. If only.

Here's what a day in the life of a so-called "fucking expert" actually looks like:

I wake up to a dozen emails with subject lines like "HELP! My wife won't fuck me anymore!!!" and "Is it cheating if I ONLY fantasize about the babysitter?" (For some reason, there is nearly always an excessive, frantic usage of caps and exclamation points which stresses me the fuck out.)

Mixed in are the classics:

"How do I last longer? PLEASE tell me!"

"Does size REALLY matter??"

And my personal favorite, "How do I get my girlfriend to do anal? ANSWER THIS!"

As if I have a magic wand that makes people suddenly crave butthole adventures before breakfast.

Well, fuck me stupid. Who knew my inbox would become the confessional booth for every horny, confused, and slightly panicked soul on the internet?

Coffee in hand (with a shot of brandy if I sense a near-death by CAPPING at hand), I start my daily sweep of the site. The adult industry is a weird, unwieldy beast. It's not all glitz and endless orgasms. Not in the slightest. For me, it's mostly customer service with an unhealthy side of "ah shit, I haven't seen this fucked-up thing before."

One minute, I'm answering a heartfelt letter from a woman who's never had an orgasm; the next, I'm deleting spam for "miracle" dick pills and blocking a guy who thinks his unsolicited dick pic is the highlight of my day (Just so we're clear: it's not, and now your junk is filed under "evidence" in my "Why I Drink" folder.)

And then there's the business of "fucking" itself. How it's sold, how it's packaged, and how it's absolutely nothing like what you see on the screen. The porn world is a fantasy factory, and I'm the janitor sweeping up the glitter and lube after the shitshow's over.

I've seen it all: the "stars" who show up high, the "directors" who think "consent" is just a technicality, and the endless parade of newbies who think a cheap camcorder and a dial-up connection will make them the next Jenna Jameson.

The truth? Most of the industry is just regular people with bills to pay, hustling to make rent, and trying to keep their boundaries intact while the world wants to buy a piece of them. The "glamorous" life is mostly exhaustion, hustling for clicks, and praying your next payout clears before your server bill does.

I've watched the business shift from big studios to DIY cam girls to desperate amateurs who think a tripod and a Yahoo group will make them famous. It won't, but it might make you a target for every scary creep with a credit card.

I get letters from people who want advice on how to fuck like a pornstar, but here's the insider secret: almost nobody in porn is actually having a good time. The scenes you see? They're choreographed, lit, and edited to look hot, but the reality is hours of awkward positions, fake moans, and "cut, reset, do it again."

I've heard from performers who faked every orgasm, from webmasters who burned out on pop-ups and piracy, and from fans who think they're broken because their sex life doesn't look like a hardcore gang-bang reel.

By lunchtime, I'm fielding messages from people who want to know if it's "normal" to want more, less, or weirder sex than their partner. (Yes. Everyone is weird. Embrace it.) I'm also dodging the occasional angry spouse who discovered their partner's browser history and wants to know if I'm personally responsible for their marital collapse. (No, but I'm flattered you think I have that much power.)

In the afternoon, I'm chasing broken links and arguing with advertisers who think I'm just another female they can fuck over. Now it's double, you prick! And trying to write just one honest, useful answer about fucking that doesn't sound like it was written by a clinician (not a chance) or some pimply teenager on an AOL chatroom.

Somewhere in this goatfuck of a mess, I'll get a message from someone in the industry. Usually a performer, sometimes a webmaster. Burned out, strung out, or just tired of pretending that fucking for money— or selling fucking for money—is always a party. It's not. It's work. Sometimes it's fun, sometimes it's soul-sucking, and sometimes it's just another Thursday.

By day's end, I've answered a dozen questions, deleted twice as many spam comments, and probably ruined someone's fantasy by telling the truth: fucking is messy, complicated, and nothing like the "movies. But it's also real. Sometimes, when you get past the bullshit and the scripts and the expectations, it's actually pretty damn great.

And that's a day in the life. Not glamorous, not tragic. Just real. And if you're lucky, a little bit funny, too.

And that's just Thursday.

Tomorrow? Who knows? Maybe I'll finally get through my inbox without a single dick pic. (Yeah, and maybe I'll get through the day without needing my magic wand for "stress relief.")

Sexual Myths I'd Like to Strangle

... the G-spot: total bullshit

> *Eh, who needs it? It doesn't even*
> *exist. — TechChick*

You can't write a sex book and skip the G-spot. The backlash from such a grave omission would be more than I could deal with. Trust me, the angry mail would bury me alive.

So here it is: my obligatory G-spot page. Please, don't write to me about what a loser I am for not saying something profound or enlightening.

Personally, I think the G-spot is a bunch of bullshit hype invented by some overzealous feminist think tank to make men feel inadequate for not finding it and make the rest of us feel like failures for not having fireworks every time someone pokes around in there.

I pay the penalty for having such views; you can bet on it. I get letters from the G-spot cult ever so often, proudly informing me of their mind-blowing, out-of-this-world, galaxy-shattering orgasm, thanks to their 'glorious' G-spot:

"Mind-blowing! Life-changing! I saw stars! The G-spot is REAL!"

TC comments: Yep, ok lady, sure thing, I believe ya, that's just great, oki dokie.

Look, I don't have the answers. A certified "sex expert" once sent me a whole rant about how ignorant I was. Her excerpt is below. I read it. Still didn't help.

TECHCHICK FACT DROP

The G-spot wasn't even named until 1981. The term hit pop culture in 1982 with a bestselling book and instantly became the most hyped "maybe-it's-real, maybe-it's-not" zone in sex history. Decades later, scientists are still arguing about whether it actually exists or if it's just the clitoris playing dress-up.

Sexpert Email Excerpt:

When she is really ready for penetration and to ensure plenty of lubrication, have your index and middle fingers lubed with K-Y or another water-based lubricant. Slowly insert your fingers into her vagina and begin exploring the entire vaginal canal, paying particular attention to the vaginal walls...

Go in as deep as she can comfortably take it and apply pressure along the length of the vaginal walls. Get a rhythm going and keep it going while applying extra pressure along the wall towards her stomach. You are stimulating her and locating the G-spot at the same time. It is located just behind the pubic bone, and you will probably feel a little ridged area. When you hit it, you will probably know by her reaction, and you want to apply an upward pressure towards her stomach by moving or cupping your fingers so you are directly stimulating her G-spot. You can kind of rock your fingers a little or move them in tight little circles, whatever feels best to her. Once you've found it, keep a steady motion going.

TC comments: Wow. Riveting stuff, and besides that... motherfucking YAWN. If you're still awake after that, congrats. You're the saint of patience.

For the record, even the scientists can't agree if the G-spot is a real thing, a cluster of nerves, or just a marketing ploy. Bottom line? If you find something that feels good, keep doing it. If not, don't sweat it.

... there's a "normal" way to have sex

Let's strangle this worst-of-all-myths on the myth-planet right out of the gate:

There is no "normal" way to have sex.
Zip. Zero. Zilch. Nada.

The only thing truly universal about sex is that everyone secretly thinks they're doing it wrong, or not doing it right enough, or often enough, or dirty enough, or "connected" enough. My god. It gives me a headache. And a heartache.

Seriously, who decided what's "normal," anyway? Some repressed Victorian ghost with a clenched jaw and a locked chastity belt? A panel of sex researchers who gave up halfway through foreplay and called it a day? Weird people, wildly off-base, and yet somehow still in charge of the narrative.

Many in the far Christian Right—secretly doing shit that should land them in jail, while condemning the rest of us to hell for simply enjoying consensual sex, defined however the fuck we choose to define it? Honestly? I hope hell is precisely what they imagined. Only they're the ones getting their asses handed to them for everything they tried to legislate away.

Newsflash: "Normal" is just a sanitized word for "what makes other people comfortable." And if you're reading me, let's be honest, you're probably not here to make anyone else feel comfortable. Bless your sex-crazed selves. I adore you.

Sex isn't a job interview. You don't have to perform it like it's going to be graded on a curve or logged in someone's highlight reel. You don't need a six-step outline, a playlist vetted by Cosmo, or a "Freaky But Not Too Freaky" scorecard to qualify.

Let me tell you what kills sex faster than six-year-old Dollar Tree lube:

Judgment. Comparison. Performance anxiety.

Wondering whether your kink makes you a freak. Wondering if you're a good lover or a bad one. Worrying your body doesn't move like it should. Feeling like you've got to orgasm in under four minutes because that's what porn and your last three partners implied was ideal.

Fuck that.

What turns you on might turn someone else completely off. What grosses you out might be someone else's Thursday night good time. And that's not weird; that's **beautifully human**.

Forget prix fixe menus and buffets. Sex isn't a restaurant. It's a potluck where everyone brings something different, and nobody's quite sure what's in the dip. And that's the fun of it.

Go for the smorgasbord—sample everything, go back for seconds, and don't be afraid to try the weird-looking stuff.

Maybe you like wax play and degradation. Maybe you just want someone to suck your toes and call you a good citizen. Maybe you want to cum while listening to Marvin Gaye. Or Beyoncé. Or whale sounds. Maybe you don't want to cum at all. Guess what? Still counts. Still sex. Still valid. Still yours.

The worst part about chasing "normal" is that it doesn't exist. It's a moving target shaped by region, religion, trends, trauma, and whatever bullshit someone with a platform decided was "sexy this season." In the 1950s, "normal" meant married, missionary, lights off, and don't make a damn sound.

By the early 2000s, "normal" was Cosmo-approved positions, bad lingerie, performative moaning, and pretending to love giving head. And depending on who you asked, anything kinkier than candlelight and eye contact still got you side-eyed or slut-shamed. Every decade redraws the line, but the myth stays the same. Both are fine.

Here's your actual sex tip:

The best sex you'll ever have happens when you stop trying to impress anyone: your partner, your past lovers, your own inner critic. Just chase what feels good. Loud or quiet. Fast or slow. Vanilla or fucked up beyond recognition. As long as it's consensual, safe, and honest? You're doing it right.

Bottom line:
Normal is a setting on your dryer. Not your sex life. Embrace your weird. Unpack your kink. Stop comparing your orgasms to somebody else's edited highlight reel.

And if anyone tries to tell you you're doing it wrong? Tell them to mind their own fucking business and go buy a magnifying mirror at the Dollar Tree. **That's the only reflection they need.**

... masturbation is only for the lonely

Masturbation is not a backup plan. It's not a sad little substitute for people who can't get laid. It's not a cry for help or a red flag or a moral failing. It's fucking masturbation. It's glorious.

But somewhere along the way, society decided that jerking off or rubbing one out was a sign that something must be wrong with you.

Too single. Too awkward. Too desperate.

Or—god forbid—a woman who enjoys her body without permission.

TECHCHICK FACT DROP

The world's oldest-known sex toy, a stone dildo, dates back over 28,000 years. Proof that even cave women weren't waiting around for Prince Fucking Charming.

There's a reason every shitty high school insult included the word masturbator. As if taking ownership of your own orgasm was something to be ashamed of. As if being able to get yourself off without begging someone else for attention was a downgrade.

Here's the truth:
People in relationships masturbate.
People in good relationships masturbate.
People in no relationship masturbate.
People who just had sex ten minutes ago might still sneak in a solo round before bed.
Yes, even monkeys masturbate.
You masturbate.
I masturbate. *A. Lot.*

Because guess what?
Sometimes you want to be selfish.
Sometimes you want something your partner doesn't offer.
Sometimes your partner's out of town. Or annoying. Or unconscious. Or maybe you just want to cum fast and dirty without making it a committee project.

Masturbation is how you learn your body.
It's how you know what works when someone else shows up. It's your laboratory, your rehearsal space, your orgasmic sandbox.

And honestly? Sometimes it's better than partnered sex. No negotiation. No misfires. No weird breath on your neck.

Lonely? Please.

Masturbation isn't lonely. It's luxury.

It's privacy, power, and pure fuck-you autonomy.

It's the one place where nobody can judge you, disappoint you, or ruin the moment with an unsolicited nipple pinch.

Bottom line:

You don't need a partner to have sex.

You are your own sex life.

And anyone who tries to shame you for that is just mad they don't cum as hard as you do.

Now, excuse me while I go get myself off.

... sex is only for the young

Let's strangle this myth with a pair of granny panties and call it a day.

The idea that sex is only for the young is pure, unfiltered bullshit. The only people who believe this are the ones who've never talked to their grandparents, or who still think "old people" are just waiting to die in a La-Z-Boy while watching reruns of M*A*S*H.

Here's the truth:

People have sex at every age. In fact, research shows that over half of people aged 65–80 are still getting it on, and most say it's a major source of happiness and life satisfaction. And guess what? They don't care about frequency. They care about enjoying it, adapting to what feels good, and not giving a damn about what anyone else thinks.

How fucking refreshing. If younger generations could say the same, I wouldn't be writing this book, "sex educators" wouldn't have jobs, the Christian Far Right would've spontaneously combusted by now, and no wars would be started by sexually frustrated dictators.

The myth that "hot sex" is only for the under-40 crowd? That's just marketing and ageism teaming up to sell you wrinkle cream and shame.

Real talk:
"Sexy" isn't an age, it's an attitude.

"Great sex" isn't a number; it's about confidence, communication, and creativity. (Which, plot twist, get better with age, not worse.)

Older adults have more sexual confidence and less shame than most twenty-somethings. They know what they want; they're less self-conscious. And they're way less likely to fake it just to stroke someone's ego.

And let's talk about variety. Older people are out here redefining what sex even means: more kissing, more touching, more experimenting, and more "let's just do what feels good and not pull a hamstring." They're not worried about Cosmo's "52 Positions Before You're 30" checklist. They're too busy actually enjoying themselves.

The real tragedy? This myth makes people dread aging, and it makes older adults feel invisible or broken when they're anything but. It also keeps doctors and therapists from talking about sexual health with older patients, which means real problems go untreated and real pleasure goes unexplored.

Bottom line:
If you think sex is only for the young, you're missing out on the best-kept secret in the bedroom.

Great sex is for anyone who wants it, at any age, in any body, for as long as you damn well please.

And if you're lucky enough to get old, may you have the kind of sex life that makes your kids, and your grandkids blush, and your friends jealous.

Now, excuse me while I go order a case of lube for my retirement plan. And not from fucking Dollar Tree.

... anal sex doesn't count as real sex

Let's get this out of the way: If it involves two (or more) consenting adults, gets your heart racing, and leaves you needing a shower, it's sex. Anal, oral, vaginal, whatever—if you're getting naked and swapping fluids, you're on the field, not the sidelines.

The idea that anal sex is somehow "not real sex" is one of the most persistent and hilarious myths out there. If you're using your body to give and get pleasure, it's sex. Full stop. The only people who say otherwise are purity-culture weirdos, loophole-hunting teens, and people who still think "virginity" is a medical diagnosis.

Why does this myth stick around?

Because some folks want to police what "counts" as sex (usually to keep you scared, ashamed, or clinging to the label "pure").

Because porn and pop culture often frame anal as something on the sidelines—an "add-on" instead of a real option for pleasure and connection.

Because, let's be honest, people get weird about butts.

Here's the truth: Anal sex is just as "real" as any other kind of sex. It's intimate, it's vulnerable, it can be mind-blowing, and yes, it can get messy (that's what towels and showers are for). It can be a main course, a side dish, or dessert... hell, maybe brunch. (Don't knock brunch.) It counts.

And for the record, people of all genders and orientations enjoy anal play. It's not just for gay men, not just for pornstars, and not just for "adventurous" couples. If you've got a butt, you're eligible. If you like it, you're normal. If you don't, you're still normal.

Also, let's kill the idea that anal sex is somehow "safer" or "doesn't count" for things like STIs or cheating. You can absolutely get STIs from anal sex, sometimes even more easily than vaginal sex, so use protection and don't fall for the "loophole" myth.

Bottom line:
If you're having fun, it's real sex. If you're not, you're doing it wrong.

And if anyone tries to tell you anal doesn't count, tell them TechChick said to get their head out of their ass and maybe put something else up there instead.

The Fetish Files

... kink & culture, what a clusterfuck

*The only thing more American
than apple pie is pretending
you're not into something weird.*
— TechChick

Americans are famously uptight about sex, especially the kinky kind. You can call yourself progressive all day, but that doesn't mean shit when it comes to being open-minded about sex. And Americans are living, breathing proof. For a country that claims to be so progressive, we're still clutching our pearls over anything that isn't missionary with the lights off.

Compare us to Europeans, who treat nudity like it's just another Tuesday and discuss kink over coffee, and it's honestly a little embarrassing.

But here's the kicker: we're obsessed with kink. We can't stop Googling it, whispering about it, or secretly wishing we were brave enough to try it.

We're fascinated by what everyone else is doing behind closed doors, but terrified to admit what we want ourselves. It's the car wreck mentality—horrified, but unable to look away.

We shake our heads at "kinky sex freaks" with disgust and pity, while our hearts (and loins) go thump-thump with envy and curiosity. And sex workers can take that fact to the bank, over and over. (If envy were currency, I'd be rich just watching their deposit slips.)

The truth? Kink isn't some fringe thing reserved for leather-clad weirdos in windowless basements. It's everywhere. Odds are, someone at your last PTA meeting has a ball gag in their nightstand.

Some studies say half the population has at least one non-vanilla interest. And that's just from the people willing to admit it in a study about "deviant" behavior.

That means your neighbor, your boss, your grandma's bridge partner, someone you know is into something you'd never guess. And what counts as "kinky" is totally subjective: for some, it's handcuffs and spanking; for others, it's just talking dirty or wanting to be tied up and told what to do, like the naughty little creatures we all are, deep down.

Here's the real clusterfuck: Americans are obsessed with labeling and judging what turns people on, but we're also desperate to be accepted for our own secret cravings. We want to peek behind the curtain, but we're utterly terrified someone might peek behind ours.

So, welcome to the Fetish Files, a tour through the wild, weird, and wonderful world of kink. Some of these stories are mine, some are from friends (thanks, Iceman), and some are just too good not to share. Whether you're a seasoned kinkster or just "kink-curious," you're in the right place. No shame, no judgment, just real talk, a little education, and a lot of "holy shit, people actually do that?!"

So, unzip your pants or your mind. Shit's about to get wonderfully weird.

... ropes & toys, PhD-level

...the kink that ties it all together

The only time I had a rope around my body was when I was six and couldn't jump rope for shit. Coordination? Not my kink. So for this one, I called in Iceman, resident rope nerd and the guy who knows his way around both curtain cord and a remote vibe.

TechChick Note: Before you even think about tying someone up, make sure you know your partner—and your knots—really well. Otherwise, you're one cocky tug away from a panicked ER visit, never being able to have a rope in your house again, including that old crusty one in your garage, and a story you'll never live down.

Iceman's Take (abridged and TechChick'd): So, you want to spice things up with toys, without getting them thrown at your head? Here's the move: tie her up first, then bring out the toys. (Kidding. Mostly.)

Step one: Get the right rope. No bungee cords. No grungy shoelaces. Go to the fabric store and buy curtain cord. It's smooth, shiny, sturdy, and doesn't leave rope burns that she'll have to explain at her book club. Practice on yourself first or prepare to spend the night apologizing to what looks like a sexy macramé project gone terrifyingly wrong.

119

Step two: Start with heavy foreplay, because nothing kills the mood like jumping straight to "hostage situation." Bind her hands behind her back. Pull the bindings snug, not tight; this is erotic restraint, not amateur hour. Then work the rope down her thighs. Japanese knots look cool and feel secure, but don't go so tight you cut off circulation. (Unless you're into amputee sex, in which case... never mind.)

Step three: Once she's bound and squirming, it's toy time. Think an inflatable butt plug, a remote-controlled vibrator, and plenty of lube. Use it everywhere. Tease, insert, and keep the vibe off at first. Anticipation is half the fun. A little clit play, a little nipple action, then slide in the butt plug. Inflate slowly. Lock it in place.

Now comes the mindfuck. Sit in a chair. Open an erotic story. Read it to her. Randomly flick the vibrator on and off. Let her twitch. Let her need. When she moans in protest, walk over, smack her ass (consensually, of course), and whisper something mean, but hot. This is your game. She's just the willing victim.

Leave the room. Let her simmer. Let her anticipate. Let her wonder what's coming next and why she's already dripping for it. Then come back, untie her, strip everything off, and take what's yours.

TC Debrief:
Am I wet, or did I just piss myself? Honestly, it's all a blur down there. Either way, Iceman's got me rethinking my position on rope. And also, my position IN rope.

Bottom line:
Communicate. Negotiate. Have safety scissors nearby. And don't forget aftercare, unless you're also into crying.

Start slow. Keep it hot. And remember: it's only kinky the first time.

... one CEO's escape plan

The only thing harder than being in charge all day is begging to give it up at night.

Dear TC,

I'm a 42-year-old Fortune 500 exec, husband, father, pet wrangler, and full-time decision machine. I make choices all day long: for my team, my boss, my wife, my kids, and whoever's goldfish just died. When it comes to sex, I don't want to lead. I don't want to initiate. I want to lay back, shut my brain off, and surrender. I want her to take control. Problem is... she's not that kind of woman. How do I turn a submissive wife into a dominant one?

Sincerely, Bill T.

Dear Bill,

First of all: you're not broken. You're exhausted. And you are absolutely not alone.

Millions of men feel exactly like you, successful on paper, respected by everyone, quietly crushed by the pressure to always be "on." To be dominant in the boardroom, in the bedroom, and in every other goddamn room, it's a trap and you're not weak for wanting out.

Wanting to submit doesn't make you less of a man. It makes you a human with a nervous system.

Now, can you turn your wife into a domme? That depends. Some people are wired for dominance. Some aren't. But just like you learned how to do taxes and tolerate small talk at networking events, dominance is a skill, and it can be learned, at least a little.

So let's talk about how to make that happen.

Domination ≠ Bondage (but they can fuck)
Don't confuse domination with tying someone up and railing them. That's bondage. Domination is about control: mental, emotional, and sexual. Sometimes they overlap, sometimes they don't, but the real power is in the mindfuck: her telling you what to do, making you wait, making the decisions while you squirm under the weight of not making them.

That's what submission is about: freedom from responsibility, in the safest, sexiest way possible. And guess what? The submissive is the one with the real power. She can only dominate if you let her. That's the game, and the beauty of it.

How to bring it up without ruining dinner
Start small. A good entry point is reading this letter with her. If she's open to it, it might spark curiosity or questions. Don't frame it as "fixing a problem." Frame it as an experiment, a fun, dirty twist on your dynamic. Hell, she might've been waiting for the moment you finally shut up and let her drive.

Be specific. "I want to surrender. I want you to tell me what to do. I want to please you, and be denied until I've earned it." Let her know what turns you on about the idea.

Then give her space to respond, without pressure. It's not about turning her into Mistress Whiplash overnight. It's about inviting her into power.

SIDEBAR: What If She's Just Not Into It?

Look, not everyone is wired for dominance, and that's okay. If your partner isn't feeling the domme vibe, don't force it or guilt-trip her. There are still plenty of ways to play with power that don't require a leather catsuit and a riding crop.

Try roleplay (boss/assistant, teacher/student, interrogator/prisoner, whatever gets you both going), switch up who leads in bed, or experiment with scripts and fantasies where she can dip a toe in without diving headfirst. Sensory play, service submission, and even just taking turns giving and receiving can scratch that itch for control and surrender.

Bottom line: Power play is about trust, not performance. If her flavor of "in charge" looks different from yours, celebrate it or get creative together. There's no one right way to play.

If she's willing to try it...

She doesn't have to go full dominatrix, just step into the role for a night, a scene, or a single command. Sometimes the hottest power play is just a whispered order and a look that says, "You're mine."

For the woman taking control:

Confidence is everything. You can't hesitate. He'll feel it, and it'll kill the mood.

No questions. No 'Do you like this?' or 'Should I keep going?' You decide. He obeys. (Check in after, not during.)

Talk dirty, but with authority. Tell him what to do. Praise or punish. Draw it out. Deny him. Reward him after he's earned it.

It's not about pain. It's about control. Make him wait. Make him serve. Make him ache for permission.

And always, always check in after. Dominance and submission can hit deep. So does being seen and held when it's over.

Final word: This isn't about becoming a full-time dom/sub couple, unless you want to. It's about balance. Relief. And reclaiming the part of sex that makes you feel something again.

And if she's not into it? You're still a badass for asking. Now go pour yourself a drink and enjoy not making a single decision for the next ten minutes.
— **TC**

... the forbidden fantasy

Dangerous Desires? Why the Rape Fantasy Exists

A look at one of the most misunderstood (and misjudged) sexual fantasies: what it is, what it isn't, and why it shows up in the minds of people who would never dream of harming anyone.

This is the one section where I'm dropping the snark. If you're reading this and feeling nervous, you're not alone. This is about honesty, not shock value.

Let's talk about the "rape fantasy," also called consensual non-consent (CNC).

If you've ever fantasized about being overpowered, "taken," or forced into sex, you're in very large, very normal company. Numerous authoritative studies, including published research in major sex journals, confirm that these fantasies are among the most common, especially for women.

(If you need to pick your jaw up off the floor, now's the time.)

If you're feeling unsettled, you're not alone. But let's be clear: there's a world of difference between fantasy and reality.

Why does this happen? There's no single answer. Some psychologists say this fantasy is about surrender, giving up control in a world that demands you always have it. Others say it's about exploring taboo, or the thrill of being so desired that someone "can't help themselves." For some, it's a way to process fear, trauma, or simply to play with power in a safe, controlled way. For many, it's just what turns them on, and that's enough.

But let's be absolutely clear:

Having a rape fantasy does **not** mean you want to be harmed, violated, or abused in real life.

CNC play (consensual non-consent) is only safe, sane, and sexy when everyone involved negotiates, agrees on boundaries, uses safe words, and checks in before, during, and after.

Fantasy is a private, controlled space. In reality, consent is everything. There's a world of difference between "I want to be taken" in a fantasy and "I want to be violated" in life. If that sounds confusing or blurry, stop here. Go learn the difference before you even fantasize about playing it out.

If you're curious about this fantasy:

Talk openly with your partner.

Set clear boundaries and safe words.

Check in before, during, and after.

Only play with people you trust deeply.

If you're a survivor of sexual violence and have these fantasies: You are not broken. You are not "asking for it." Many survivors report these fantasies, and for some, they existed before any trauma. If you're struggling, please seek support from a trauma-informed therapist or counselor.

Bottom line: You're not alone. You're not broken. You're not bad. Fantasy is where we get to play with the edges of our desires, safely and on our own terms. If you're going to play with fire, do it with your eyes open, your boundaries clear, and your trust unshakable.

... spanking 101 (not!)

Anyone can slap an ass. It takes skill to make her actually beg for it. And yes, I've begged for it. Maybe, just maybe, that's thanks to Mr. Smith, yes, real name, my 7th grade Science Teacher, who used to haul me into the hall and paddle my butt every time I acted up. I was a hottie in 7th grade. I acted up a lot.

But looking back, two things bug the ever-loving shit out of me: First, isn't 13 a fuckton-old to be paddling? And second, why the hell did my parents think it was just fine to send me to a school where I didn't learn shit and corporal punishment was just a dandy idea?

TechChick Note: If you're going to try spanking, don't just wing it. Consent isn't optional. Talk about it first: what's hot, what's off-limits, what's a hard no, and what's a "hell yes." Set boundaries, agree on safe words, and check in before, during, and after. If she's not into it, you're about to find out what a real slap feels like.

Iceman's Take (abridged & TechChick'd): So you want to give a spanking that's more than a quick smack in the heat of the moment? Here's how to do it right:

Step 1: Gather Your Tools
You don't need a dungeon. But if you want to go all out, here's the shopping list:

Handcuffs (or something soft to tie with)

Suede and leather floggers (start soft, work up)

Aloe vera lotion and a tray of ice cubes

And above all, a confident, take-charge attitude

Step 2: Set the Scene
Start when things are already hot. Find a playful "reason" to take control; maybe she's been "bad," maybe she just looks too damn good. Take her hands, cuff them behind her back, and let her know you're in charge (but keep it gentle unless you've mutually agreed to rougher play).

Step 3: Position and Tease
Lay her face down, get her up on her knees, and make sure her ass is front and center. Touch is everything: slow, strong moves that say you're in control. If you have a crop, use it to gently part her legs. Here's the deal: drag it across her clit for instant cooperation. No crop? Hands work fine. Just be slow and firm. And don't forget: spanking without clit or pussy play is just a spanking. Keep her turned on.

Step 4: Warm Up

Start with the suede flogger. Use a soft, fanning motion to warm up her ass and get the blood flowing. Think gentle, not punishment. Silence is golden here; let her sighs do the talking. When her skin glows pink, grab an ice cube and trace slow circles over her ass and pussy. The hot/cold contrast is a game-changer. Keep up the clit and pussy stimulation. This is supposed to be pleasure, not punishment.

Step 5: Level Up

Ask if she's learned her lesson. If not, it's time for the leather flogger. This one stings, so go slow. Use figure-eight motions or simple slaps, but keep it controlled. Watch her reactions: red and warm is good; grimacing means back off. Alternate with more ice for extra sensation and to keep welts at bay. And yes, keep her pussy and clit in play. Otherwise, it's just a sore ass.

Step 6: Aftercare & Finish

When her ass is glowing, use a towel to dry her off, then rub in a cooling aloe vera lotion, firm but gentle. This soothes the sting and keeps the play feeling good. Aftercare isn't optional: cuddle, check in, and make sure she feels safe and adored. If you want, finish with a hard slap and a final "lesson." Or, if you're both ready, move on to sex. She'll be extra sensitive, and you'll both be fired up. Better yet: let her sit on your face for some well-deserved pussy eating (her on top, her ass will thank you). Or let her ride you, she controls the pace, and you get the view.

TC comments: Lord help me, I need... ummmm... a break. Or maybe just a really good spanking. Hard to tell.

... i cum, you cum, we all cum

Threesomes. Moresomes. Once "fringe," now just another fantasy on the menu.

Let's not kid ourselves: the number one fantasy for men is two women, one him, all naked and going at it like a pack of wild animals. How do you make it happen? Hell if I know for sure, but here's what I've learned:

The "Easy" Way (It's Not *Really* Easy)
First, your partner has to be open-minded. If she's strictly vanilla, save your breath (and your relationship) and move on to the "hard way" below.

If she's got a little curiosity, start slow. Talk about sex, a lot. Share your fantasies, your turn-ons, and your "wouldn't it be wild if..." thoughts. The trick? Make it clear you don't want another woman—you want the experience. And if you think she's open to a little girl-on-girl play (trust me, more women are than you'd guess), tell her you'd love to see her with another woman. That way, she gets to explore her own curiosity, and you get a front-row seat. Win-win.

But here's the golden rule: She picks the other woman. Don't push for someone hotter, younger, or who makes her feel insecure. If you do, you'll be jerking off alone for a long, long time.

If you're lucky and she agrees, remember, this is her show. Stay a spectator until you're invited in. Don't charge in with your dick out like a frat boy at a kegger. Slow your roll, read the room, and only join when you're damn sure you're wanted.

If you're both into it but nervous? Hire a pro. She'll break the ice, keep things smooth, and make sure nobody's left out or freaked out. But remember: no trust, no threesome. Period.

The "Hard" Way

If your partner's not interested, your only real option? Hire a pro through a reputable escort agency and set up your own fantasy: safely, discreetly, and without dragging anyone into something they don't want.

If the fantasy only works when it's her in the mix, you're not chasing a threesome, you're chasing connection. And that's a whole different game.

Final TechChick Wisdom

This is a tough one to pull off. If it happens, count your lucky stars and don't fuck it up by getting greedy.

If it doesn't happen, you're not broken or missing out on the meaning of life. Most fantasies are better in your head than in a messy, real-life bed anyway.

If you're going to try it, keep your ego in check, your expectations realistic, and your sense of humor fully engaged.

More on the lesbian thing next page... trust me, you'll want to read on.

... girl-on-girl dreams

Ever wonder how to pull off a threesome without the drama, disaster, or drunken crying? I was lucky enough to get a guest contributor who calls herself a threesome expert and after reading what happened, I believe her.

She gifted her boyfriend the ultimate fantasy: a night with her, another woman, and zero rules. What happened next? I'll let her tell it. (Grab a towel)

She begins:
The whole thing was one of the most sensual, erotic, and downright filthy experiences of my life. The three of us met in a hotel bar. I was twenty minutes late and extremely nervous about both being late and what lay ahead, but when I walked in, I saw them in a back booth: my man, and this woman who looked like pure sex in heels. We drank, flirted, drank more, flirted more, and I couldn't keep my eyes off her. She oozed heat and fuck-me confidence. I knew I was in for something seriously wild.

We all got properly warmed up in that bar and by the time we got upstairs, we were already halfway to fucking. The second the door shut, she was on me, arms around my waist, her lips brushing my ear, whispering all the filthy things she wanted to do. My heart was pounding, my panties were soaked, and I melted back into her, letting her take the lead. I completely surrendered.

My guy sprawled out on the sofa, eyes wide, already hard as a rock. But honestly, I forgot he was even there. She spun me around and kissed me, deep and hungry, her hands everywhere, undressing me while we were still standing. I was naked before I knew it, and I couldn't stop staring at her body as she stripped, slow and teasing, each move making my skin tingle with unbearable anticipation.

We pressed into each other, hands exploring, mouths devouring. Her kisses were soft and warm, but her hands were pure fire, moving over every inch of my skin. She pushed me back onto the bed and took her time, kissing, licking, and sucking every inch of me until I was trembling, breathless, desperate for more. When she finally slid her mouth down to my pussy, I nearly lost my mind. Her tongue was relentless: soft, then firm, flicking my clit, then plunging deep, her fingers curling inside me just right. I was dripping, soaked through, and she devoured every drop like she'd been starving for every thick, creamy drop of my cum.

She brought me to the kind of orgasm that makes you see stars, my whole body shaking, legs quivering, hands tangled in her hair as I cried out for more. When I finally came down, my boyfriend had slipped into the bed with us, but my mind was still on her, every nerve ending still buzzing from her mouth and hands.

The three of us fucked and sucked for hours, bodies tangled, mouths and hands everywhere, no rules, just raw, hungry pleasure. But honestly, she was the star of the show. When it was all over, I could barely stand. My body was weak, my mind completely blown.

As I was leaving, she caught me in the lobby, walked me outside, and pressed me against my car. She kissed me again, slow and sweet and filthy as hell. Then she slipped me her number and disappeared into the night like a damn movie scene. We hooked up for more wild sex after that, and my sex life with my boyfriend? Never better.

TC: Well, holy-fuckshit-Christ. If you're not dripping after that, check your pulse. No, really.

Bottom line:
Girl-on-girl dreams aren't just a male fantasy. Sometimes, the hottest thing a woman can ever do is let another woman take her apart, piece by trembling piece, while he watches and learns how it's really done.

... toy box extraordinaire

> **TECHCHICK FACT DROP**
>
> In Alabama and Mississippi, it's still illegal to buy a vibrator in a shop. But you can own a gun. Priorities, y'all.

Women love their toys. And why the hell wouldn't we? They're empowering, efficient, and completely under our control.

See this little vibe? Look what it does to me. I've got orgasms on demand, no questions asked.

It's not about replacing anyone. It's about taking your pleasure into your own damn hands.

Now, let's talk about the men.

Some of you look at toys like competitors in a dick-measuring contest you didn't sign up for.

At first, you might pretend not to care: "Sure, babe, whatever gets you off..."

But the first time you see a vibrator send your partner into a body-melting, clit-screaming blackout? You get quiet. Like reevaluating-your-life-choices quiet.

Listen up:
Do. Not. Get. Jealous.
The toy is your wingman. It's not the enemy.

No vibrator has ever whispered sweet nothings, eaten her leftovers, or made her laugh during a horror movie.
She's not falling in love with it.

She's getting hornier for you, and you get to watch her unravel like a goddamn miracle.

It's not competition. It's pregame.

Here's the game plan:

If it's your first time adding a toy to the mix, keep it simple.

The clit rules.

Start with a basic vibe. Small, quiet, non-intimidating.

No need to strap a 15-speed jackhammer to her pelvis on day one. Save the heavy artillery for later. Think entry-level: battery-powered, slender, no USB port required.

And please: DO NOT SKIMP.

No K-Mart knockoffs. No dollar-store batteries.

You don't want that thing dying right before liftoff because you cheaped out on Energizer.

Don't yank batteries out of your kid's toy truck, either. (Yes, I see you.)

Invest like you're building a future. Because you are. One orgasm at a time.

Now the fun part:

You're in the heat of foreplay. She's writhing. It's time.

Don't just jam it on her clit like a novice. Tease her. Let it glide across her nipples, belly, thighs, everywhere but where she wants it.

Build the tension. Hold the line until her whole body says yes.

And when she does?

Give it to her, slow, steady, focused.

Watch what happens next.

She'll take over. Her hips will roll, her moans will rise, and your role will shift to "lucky son of a bitch who gets to witness this masterpiece."

By the time she's shaking, soaked, and wrecked in the best way possible, she'll pull you into her like it's instinct.

And when you fuck her then?
She will never look at you the same again.
And that's a very, very good thing.

One last note:
If she ever names the toy, like:
"Come here, my itty bitty little wittle Slim Jimmy Jim, and give your mama what she needs..."

Take it out to the shooting range. With love. And hollow points.

... this little piggy went to...

> There is no unhappier creature
> on earth than a fetishist who
> yearns for a woman's shoe and
> has to embrace the whole woman.
> — Karl Kraus, Austrian Writer
> and Satirist

I just love that quote. Totally nailed it.

Ready for some wild and wacky inbox reading?

Q: Do most women enjoy giving foot jobs? And how do you think a man can convince his lady to foot-fucking him?

A: I don't know if most women enjoy it, but let's be honest, 'most women' doesn't matter. You're not trying to win a demographic; you're trying to get your partner off. So just ask. If she's into it, she'll say yes. If she's not, she'll say no. And no, you're not asking her to do deep-sea anal with no prep; it's a foot job. Keep it fun.

Q: I'm a woman who wants to jack off my hubby with my feet, but it doesn't seem all that easy. How do I do it? Is there an easy way?

A: Uh, hell if I know... just grip his dick with your feet and start moving up and down really slow until you find a rhythm. You might want to try lube or just keep it dry with a little grip, but don't go overboard with anything slippery, or your foot may land an accidental uppercut to his jaw (tempting for some, I know). And once you've got the motion, just start working it like a $10 hand job. Have fun.

Q: Do you like your feet being serviced orally? If so, what exactly do you like? Any hints for guys who like to treat female feet but don't quite know how?

A: Let's just say I don't always kiss and tell. But yep, I've had a toe or two in my mouth. If you're a newbie foot worshipper, stick to the basics: kissing, sucking, licking. Avoid tickling. Read her reactions, keep it easy at first, and only turn up the heat if she gets more into it. Like anything new, slow and steady wins the race. Think erotic, not ticklish.

Q: Do you think it's disgusting for a girl to kiss a MAN's feet, or can you think of a way to make this technique attractive to women? Or, as I can't imagine you to be a novice to anything, have you ever done it?

A: No, I don't think it's disgusting. I try to avoid words like "disgusting," "perverted," or "freaky twisted scumbag" when I'm talking about sex. I like sex. I'm kind to sex. I don't have any magic trick to make it "attractive to women." This is one of those things you just have to try and see if she calls you a freaky pig or grabs your toes and starts slurping away. And yeah, I might have kissed, licked, or sucked an occasional toe or two in my freaky lifetime.

Now, for one of my favorite foot-themed emails: a guy with a true flair for the erotic and the nasty. Fantasies like this are healthy, hot, and make sex lives awesome. The point? Whatever your thing is—feet, domination, dildo play, dressing up, fisting—don't be afraid to enjoy your fantasies and explore them. Sex gets REALLY good when fantasy and reality collide.

---- begin excerpt ----

...And I can't stop fantasizing about you naked on your back with your feet behind your head, one end of a big jelly dildo in your mouth and one in your pussy, you completely lost to your lust, and me kneeling behind your head, licking, licking, licking the soles of your feet, and mouth-fucking every single one of your toes, trying so hard as if I could make them ejaculate. I promise I would do this for hours. And if I couldn't hold my love juice anymore, I would cover your feet in it and then lick it off...

---- end excerpt ----

Moral of the Piggy Story
If you've got a "little piggy" fantasy, give zero fucks and go for it. Life's too short for boring sex, especially when there are toes to curl and boundaries to break.

... Q&A: Kinky Queries

A mixed trio of kinky shit:

Q. I have the fantasy of smelling women's used panties. I've even thought of buying one. Is there anything wrong with me?

A. I take it you're not living with anyone. Otherwise, you'd already be up to your eyeballs in used panties. No, there's nothing wrong with you. A lot of men are turned on by our scent, especially if we, uh, keep it fresh. Pussy-scented panties can be hot... just maybe not 48 hours post-workout. Bottom line? If nobody's getting hurt (without asking for it) and no one's being coerced, sniff away.

Q. My fiancée loves for me to lick, finger, and play with her navel. Sometimes she even gets off from it. I thought it was weird at first, but now I'm into it. Thoughts?

A. Totally normal. The navel can be an erogenous zone. I think the medical explanation is something like "there's a connective thingy between the belly button and the groin that can send shockwaves to the genitals." But hell, who needs a medical degree? If it gets her off, keep going.

Q. I love seeing my wife dressed like a schoolgirl, plaid skirts, white anklet socks, the whole fantasy. I've also asked her to fuck other men in front of me, but instead she went off and did it behind my back. She says it's FOR ME, but I want to witness it. Am I being unreasonable to want the outfit AND the gangbang?

A. Dude. Are you okay? Forget the socks, you've got bigger problems. She's not doing it for you. She's doing it because she wants to, and not with you in the room. She doesn't want your face anywhere near her fun. That's not fantasy. That's deception. Does that sound reasonable?

... A Day in the Life: Of Fetish

Nothing fazes me anymore.
When it comes to porn on the internet, I've seen it all. I'm desensitized. And no, that's not a flex; it's what happens when your libido takes one look and taps out.

Compared to what hits my inbox, I'm practically a nun. Even I, yes, me, have moments where I blink and say, "What the actual fuck?"

There's just something about reviewing fetish site submissions at 2 a.m. that strips the shock right out of your soul.

And still, still, I find myself whispering "Jesus Christ" to my cat while I hover over the "approve" button, wondering what the hell happened to missionary and a moan.

They submit. I review. I decide what to list based on two simple criteria:

Not overloaded with ads.

Content I think my visitors will like.

It's that second one that breaks me. Get too loose, and the hate mail floods in. Too picky? Suddenly I'm an uptight, sex-negative bitch. There's no winning in kink.

Pornstar and hardcore categories? No problem.
But "kinky"? That's where it gets dicey.

There are so many fetishes being exploited online now that I honestly think half of them didn't even exist until someone uploaded a video, and a thousand people suddenly realized it gave them a boner. Boom, fetish born.

It's shock-TV logic: once you've gone off the rails, there's no such thing as enough.
Same with porn. The question is always: how fucking weird can we go?
Reality check: there's no bottom.

I like to think I'm nonjudgmental, but after years in the trenches, I've broken fetishes down into three loose categories:

Harmless fun: "You do you, babe."

Twisted freaky: "Okay, that's... a lot, but I respect the hustle."

And Jesus Christ, who hurt you: "Therapy exists. Use it."

Once upon a time, kinky meant a little spanking, maybe a maid outfit. Now? Let me show you the timeline of descent:

Old way: a man and a woman fucking, lesbian action...
New way: clowns, amputees, nuns, grandmas, vampires, tattooed trans dommes in leather chaps on pogo sticks.

Old toy: a girl with a dildo
New toy: fruit, vegetables, crucifixes, balloon pumps, chains, machine parts, garage tools, actual candles on actual waxed genitals

Old group: threesomes
New group: orgies, gangbangs, alien sex, robot sex, possibly involving glow sticks

Old clothes: lingerie, French maid uniforms
New clothes: full latex exoskeletons that squeak when she breathes

Old shock: naked girl on a horse
New shock: girl pretending to fuck the horse and charging extra for the "chicken bonus" scene.

Old action: mild spanking
New action: face sitting, foot trampling, catfighting, lactation, fisting, piss play, and yes, scat. (That's shit. Literal shit.)

Sex has gotten so weird and so theatrical that sometimes I miss the days when missionary with the lights on could get the job done. Sigh.

And that's just Friday.
By Monday, I'm muttering "Jesus Christ" to my coffee while approving a site called **GrandmaGobblers69.**

And people wonder why I drink...

Cleanup on Aisle 69

... we all do it, don't lie

> *We all think we're sexy beasts in the moment, until we catch ourselves sniffing our own fingers like horny bloodhounds and hiding condoms like we committed a crime. — TechChick*

Let's get real: Everyone's got their own private rituals, weird little habits, and "did anyone see that?" moments in the bedroom. If you say you don't, you're either full of shit or you've never had sex with the lights on. Here's the unfiltered list of stuff we all do but pretend we don't. Go ahead, claim your weird.

Sex Habits Everyone Does But Nobody Talks About:

The Finger Sniff
You go exploring, you come up for air, and yep, you give your fingers a sniff. It's not gross, it's instinct.
You're not performing a chemical analysis; you're just confirming the moment was as filthy and amazing as it felt.
Also: there's a 50/50 chance you won't wash your hands until at least two full meals and a coffee run later. Hygiene? Barely. This is memory preservation.

The Condom Coffin
Used condom? Immediate Code Red protocol: wrap it in three layers of toilet paper, burrito it in a paper towel, Ziploc it like it's holding state secrets, then wedge it under last night's takeout trash like you're covering a murder.
And yet, every time you take out the trash, there's still that moment of what if the bag breaks?

The Public Sex Flashback
Trader Joe's. Work meeting. DMV line. Suddenly last night's reverse cowgirl slams into your frontal cortex like a porn pop-up.
You nod blankly through Q2 projections or mumble "credit or debit" while your mind's still at "oh god, right there, fuck me harder."

The DIY Sex Toy MacGyver
Your vibrator's dead. Your wand's across the room. You? Lazy and horny. Either way, suddenly your electric toothbrush, detachable showerhead, or very suggestive cucumber starts looking real solution-y. If it buzzes, pulses, or resembles a dick, it's now classified as "Plan B." We've all had our "would this work?" moment.

The Sheet Check

You finish, roll over, and immediately scan the sheets for "evidence": massive wet spots, unrecognizable WTF-and-which-one-of-us-did-that-come-from stains, or that rogue hair tie you lost three positions ago. Time for major post-sex recon: lube stains? Check. Hair a cum-disaster? Check. Underwear hanging from the ceiling fan? Check.

Because if you're not crawling around searching for your panties, your earring, and what's left of your dignity (and maybe glancing at the ceiling just in case), did you even fuck?

The Underwear Inspection

You do the post-sex underwear check: Is that lube, sweat, cum remains, or...something worse, like your dignity? You pretend you're just "straightening up," but you're really CSI-ing your own crotch.

Nobody knows what that stain is. And it's fine. Probably.

The Pube Pluck

Somewhere during the festivities, a rogue pube ended up in your mouth. Or stuck to your chest. Or dangling from your chin like a party streamer.

The extraction process is a silent panic ballet. One swift swipe, zero eye contact, pretend it never happened.

The "Did I Fart?" Paranoia

Something made a noise. Maybe it was the bed. Maybe it was you. Either way, you freeze, eyes wide. Was it a squeak? A squeal? A sneaky toot?

Look, just blame the dog. And if you don't have one, get one. Instant alibi.

The Pre-Game Sniff Test

You're heading down south and suddenly remember... you're a human. You panic-sniff your pits, your breath, and possibly your own crotch. Just in case.

This isn't vanity. It's self-preservation.

The "Was That Good?" Overthink

The sex is over. The sweat's drying. The spiral begins. Was that groan sexy or seizure-adjacent? Did your dirty talk sound hot or like bad improv? Was that gasp one of pain? You start reviewing footage that doesn't exist, frame by frame.

Relax. I mean, I know you can't... I can't. Do what I do: smoke a joint and order Taco Bell.

Wrap it Up

If you're reading this and thinking "ew, who does that?" congrats, you're the only one. The rest of us are out here folding condoms like origami, sniffing our own fingers like somms at a pussy vineyard, and pretending we didn't just check the sheets for DNA. Welcome to the club.

... bushy, bushy business

Your Bits, Your Rules

Let's get this straight: There is no "correct" pube style. There's only what makes you feel sexy, savage, and ready to ride. Bushy, bare, buzzed, or Picasso-level abstract, if it gets you in the mood and doesn't chafe, it's perfect. That whole "must be bald to be bangable" mindset? Dead. Buried. Probably got razor burn in hell.

The Big Shift: Your Style, Your Choice

Full '70s disco bush? Legendary. You're one pelvic thrust away from Studio 69.

Minimalist trim, a landing strip, or a totally bare runway? Still iconic.

Feeling creative? Hearts, lightning bolts, or a custom fade. Why not.

Dudes, you're not exempt. Manscape it, jungle it, or go bare. If it doesn't itch and doesn't stink, you're golden.

The big shift? Personal choice and comfort now matter more than any imposed trend. The only rule is: do you. Literally. Or with company.

What Actually Makes Sex Better (It's Not Just Hair)

Clean, Not Squeaky: Wash your bits with warm water and, if you must, a gentle, unscented cleanser. Skip the harsh soaps, wipes, and anything that claims to make you "smell like a cupcake." The vagina is self-cleaning, don't mess with the natural order. (Every time man messed with nature, just look where it got us!)

Don't Douche: No. Still no. Stop. Douching jacks up your pH, opens the door for infections, and earns you zero orgasms. If you're worried about odor, see a doctor, not a pop-up ad.

Post-Sex TLC: Pee after sex. Rinse off. Let your vulva breathe. You don't need a whole spa day, just don't sit there stewing in sex sweat and fluids. A simple piss will fix the pH, the funk, and whatever's brewing down there.

Lube Is Your BFF: Friction is the enemy of good sex. Use lube, especially if you're freshly shaved or waxed, to keep things smooth and avoid microtears or irritation. I once had a microtear that felt like a macrotear and no, I wasn't giving birth.

Moisturize (If You Groom): If you're going bare or near-bare, treat your crotch like it's getting ready for a red carpet. Aloe, coconut oil, vitamin E, whatever doesn't set your genitals on fire. Moisturized skin means less friction and fewer "mothafuckin' ouch" moments.

Reader Confessions / Top Grooming Fails:

Confession 1: The Patchwork Catastrophe
"I tried to do a 'quick trim' with my boyfriend's beard trimmer. Ended up with a reverse mohawk and a bald patch shaped like Australia. Still got laid, but now he calls it 'down under.'"

Confession 2: The Waxing Meltdown
"Booked a Brazilian at a cheap salon. She left me mid-strip, spread-eagle, stuck like a Thanksgiving turkey. I've never prayed so hard for a fire alarm."

Confession 3: The Chemical Burn
"Used a depilatory cream labeled 'gentle.' It was not.
I spent the night with an ice pack between my legs and a renewed spiritual commitment to letting my natural bush live its best life."

Bottom Line:
Your pubes, your rules.
If your crotch looks like a topiary, a runway, or a tiny forest of rebellion, who cares?
Keep it clean, keep it comfy, and stop grooming to please people who still think vaginas are confusing.
Confidence is sexy. Razor bumps aren't.

... pissing, farting, & uh-oh's

Sex isn't graceful. It's not cinematic. It's not whatever slow-mo bullshit perfume ads are peddlingIt's bodily chaos, sweaty, slippery, and occasionally audible in ways no one consented to.

We already touched on some of this in We All Do It, but these are the blooper reel moments that deserve their own standing ovation. If none of these have happened to you? You're either having sex with mannequins or lying to my face.

The Accidental Soundtrack (Remix)
Bodies are loud. Flesh hits flesh, skin sticks, stomachs gurgle, air gets trapped in holes it never should've entered.
You'll swear it was the bed. They'll pretend not to notice.
And you? You'll just lay there, eyes wide, reevaluating every Taco Tuesday decision you've ever made.
Lesson: Never fuck after tacos.

The Mystery Stain (Greatest Hits Edition)
You roll over and freeze.
There's... something. A wet spot the size of Kansas. A mystery splatter. A smear. Seriously?
Could be lube. Could be blood. Could be... that other thing. You don't want to know, and you're not going to ask.
You do the mature thing:
Flip the sheet, pretend you're at a hotel, and if it comes back to haunt you, upgrade to towel-life like the rest of us.
Gold-star move: sleep on the wet side without complaint.

The Golden Splash Zone
You're deep in the action, hips are moving, the moans are flowing.
And then?
A little *extra moisture* that wasn't part of the plan.
Maybe it's a sneeze. Maybe it's that second vodka soda.
Maybe it's the thrill. Maybe your pelvic floor threw in the towel mid-thrust.
No judgment: Just towel off, hydrate, and maybe don't bounce on a full bladder.

The Rogue Entry

You're aiming for home base, but the GPS reroutes. Wrong hole, wrong time, wrong everything. There's a yelp, a glare, and possibly a new rule about "announcing your intentions" combined with "What the FUCK, dude?"

Truth: If you both survive, you're either married, trauma-bonded, or at least on a first-name basis with each other's sphincter.

Crampageddon

You're seconds from climax, right as your left leg locks up like it's been hit with a taser.

One moment you're a sex god, the next you're rolling on the floor screaming about your calf.

Your partner's still riding high. You're negotiating with Satan for a new hamstring.

Recovery protocol: laugh, stretch, resume... if you still have circulation.

The Unexpected Guest Star

You're mid-thrust, fully vulnerable, when the cat jumps on the bed. Or your toddler appears.

Or your roommate yells about stolen Hot Pockets mid-thrust.

And now you're trying to yank a sheet over your naked ass while pulling out like a panicked bank robber.

You haven't known true panic until you've tried to cover up with a fitted sheet while still inside someone.

Solution: Lock the damn door. Or schedule sex like adults. Or develop an exhibitionist streak and just roll with it.

Bottom line: If your sex life is perfectly choreographed and mess-free, I don't trust you.

Real sex is hilarious. Gross. Unexpected.

And honestly? That's the fun part.

Lube leaks, cramp attacks, surprise farts: welcome to the jungle. Forget the filter. Bring a towel. And a sense of humor.

... lights off, lights on: listen, ladies

Let's talk about illumination.

When it comes to sex, men are visual. Not "they appreciate aesthetics" visual—they're porn-addled spotlight chasers who would bang under stadium lighting if it meant getting a better view.

Women, on the other hand?
We're master escape artists. We want shadows, covers, dim lighting, maybe a flickering candle four rooms away.
Basically, we want to be appreciated without actually being seen.

Not every guy is a spotlight junkie, and not every woman wants to hide. But if you're reading this, you probably know which camp you're in.

And yet, it does seem like it's always, always, always "lights on" for dudes.

Why?
Because they like what they're looking at.

Yes, even if you've got back rolls, stretch marks, or one boob that insists on migrating west while lying flat.
Men aren't squinting at your flaws.
They're hypnotized by movement, flesh, wetness, and reactions. The jiggle, the bounce, the arch. That slow pull of a thong over hips. The glisten of your skin when you're sweating and wrecked.

You think you look awkward.
He thinks he's about to nut.

Look, you can fuck in the dark for the rest of your life if you want.
But if you've ever wondered why he always "accidentally" leaves the lamp on?
Because he wants to see every goddamn second of you falling apart.

TC Confession: I used to be a lights-off girl. I'd keep a shirt on, hips angled just right, sheets bunched around whatever I was insecure about that week.

And then one night, mid-fuck, I saw him staring at me like I was a damn miracle.
I asked, "What are you looking at?"
He said, "Everything. Don't stop."

That was it.
The lights stayed on after that.

Now I ride him like a queen under full lighting, full frontal, no shame.
Not because I "fixed" my body.
But because I finally realized he was never trying to tolerate it.
He couldn't get enough, and I was the dumbass turning away like it was a flaw, not a fucking gift.

And if you really want to blow his mind?
Next time, turn the lights on yourself.
Stand there.
Naked.
Unbothered. Let him look.
Own the room. Own the moment.
And give him something to fucking stare at.

... etiquette: sex hair, regrets, & flight

Let's talk post-sex behavior.

Not the moans, the squirting, or the "was that your toe or my ribcage?" chaos. We've covered that.

This is about what happens *after* the grand finale. When the sweat's drying, the lube's leaking, and choices are being made.

And some of y'all? Making *the wrong ones*.

Sex Hair Isn't a Look. It's a Warning Sign

If you've got bedhead that screams "I just got railed into a wall," maybe skip the mimosa brunch acting all casual.

You're not fooling anyone. We all know what you did. We just don't want to smell it in line at the bagel shop.

Fix your hair. Change your shirt. Wipe the glitter off your tits and the mascara that somehow made it to your mouth. You don't need to do a full red-carpet beat, just try not to look like you left your dignity in a stranger's sheets.

The "Post-Nut Regret Spiral"

You came. It was hot. It was maybe too fast. And now you're lying there wondering if you just let a human thumb raw-dog you for mediocre reasons.

Here's the deal:

Regret is temporary. Bad dick is forever.

Learn your lesson, hydrate, and block the number.

And if it wasn't that bad? Stop spiraling. You had sex.

Congrats. You're still a functioning animal with a pulse.

If you're not cringing at least once a year, you're not living.

The Houdini (aka The Post-Fuck Flight Risk)

You don't need to stay the night. No one's asking for spooning under a weighted blanket while you whisper your childhood trauma.

But don't be that asshole who cums, zips, and vanishes like a Craigslist ghost.

Say a word. Any word. "Thanks" works. "Later" is fine. "That was fun" if you want to seem human.

We're not looking for breakfast; we're looking for basic fucking manners.

(Unless you shot your wad at our place. And we allowed you to stay. In that case, yes, you're buying bagels.)

Bottom line: There's no sex etiquette manual, but if there were, it wouldn't include fleeing, fake amnesia, or nutting into the void and disappearing like you're in witness protection.

Clean up after yourself. Don't leave your partner questioning their life choices. And for the love of all things holy, say goodbye before you bolt.

... Q&A: Really Random

Let's be honest: the sex part is usually the easy part. It's the before, the after, and the WTF-just-happened in between that get people spiraling. Should you say something? Should you fake something? Should you apologize for crying, or accidentally calling them "daddy" in the wrong tone?

These are the moments Google can't save you from. So here you are, asking TechChick.

Good. You should.

Q: Is porn wrong? My girlfriend thinks I'm being a pervert for looking at naked women. I tell her I truly enjoy it.

A: Let's be real: if watching porn is wrong, then half the planet is going straight to horny jail. Look, I'm literally in the business, so obviously I don't think porn is the devil's work. But here's the real deal: a lot of women get their panties in a twist because it feels like they're competing with a pornstar who's got a whole crew, lighting, and a script. It's not about you; it's about the fantasy.

So, if your girl's feeling insecure, don't just wave it off. Reassure her she's the star of your real-life show, not some pixelated extra. And hey, maybe keep your browser history clear and your VHS stash out of sight, not because you're ashamed, but because you respect her feelings. Bottom line: porn isn't evil, but hiding it like you're twelve is just sad. Own your kinks, but don't be a dick about it.

Q: When my girlfriend cums it is really watery, tastes salty, and smells a lot like piss. I've never tasted piss before so this may be normal, or not. TC, I always thought it was supposed to be creamy... am I right?

A: What are you feeding her, a urinating grouper? If it's overpowering, funky, or suddenly smells like something died, maybe suggest a hygiene check or a quick trip to the gyno. Otherwise? Keep your mouth where it's happy and healthy, and remember: there's no one recipe for "delicious." *Sex is messy, not some neat little snack platter.*

Q: My wife of 14 years just confessed that before we were married, she slept with more than 200 guys. I love her to death, but I'm having a tough time dealing with this. Any advice?

A: Ah, the classic double standard: he's a stud, she's a slut. Here's the truth: what happened before you met her is ancient history. You love her now, right? Then focus on that.

Think of it this way: she's been around the block, knows what she likes, and that makes her a damn good lover. Plus, she picked you out of a crowd of 200. That's the real flex. So, chest out, pride on, and maybe buy her some flowers. And if you're still spiraling, ask yourself why you're threatened by her past instead of grateful for her present.

Q: How do I actually ask for what I want in bed without sounding needy or weird?

A: You just ask. No PowerPoint, no rehearsed speech, no apologizing for wanting good sex.

Try something simple like, "Hey, I love it when you do X; can we do more?" or "I want to try something new; are you in?"

If they make you feel weird for asking, they're the problem, not you.

The only thing weirder than asking for what you want is pretending you don't want anything at all. Closed mouths don't get fed; or fucked the way they want.

Bottom line: If you're spiraling about something weird, awkward, or "should I say this?" in bed, you're not alone. The real secret? Say the thing. Ask the thing. Laugh at the thing. If you don't feel at least a little awkward, congrats—you're officially a robot. Which means you probably scanned this book in 1.8 seconds.

And honestly? That scares me. A lot.

... A Day in the Life: Odds & Ends

Wake up, stretch, and spot a suspicious bruise shaped like New Jersey on my thigh.

Make coffee. Spill half of it down my shirt. Decide it's fashion.

Get interrupted by a spam call from "IRS Collections." Realize halfway through the call my shirt's on inside out and there's a condom wrapper stuck to my sock.

Field a call from my mom: "Are you seeing anyone nice?" Pause. "Define 'nice,' Mom."

Spend 20 minutes searching for my phone, which is in my hand.

And then, just like that, the noise quiets.

I remember an email I haven't answered yet. She says, "I just got divorced, and I don't know how to have sex anymore. I don't know how to be touched."

Sometimes I forget this isn't all performance. That behind the kinks and chaos and condom socks are real people. Hurting, healing, hoping for something better than the last mess. Sex isn't just a game we play. It's how some of us survive. It's the only time we feel seen.

For others, though, they forget how to be seen, how to have sex, or even how to be touched.

I answer her. Carefully. Slowly. Like I'm untying a knot.

"Start small," I write. "Start where it doesn't hurt. You don't have to be anyone but yourself. That's enough."

And maybe that's all we ever needed to hear.

Then I go back to writing a column about farting during anal. Balance.

And then it's on to writing a whole sex advice column about how to exit after sex without being a dick... then I realize I haven't exited my apartment in 36 hours.

Field another call from my mom: "I meant to ask, how's that *'tech startup'* going, dear?" Pause. "I quit *'that job'* last month, Mom."

And somewhere in the middle of all that chaos, I remember:
This is the good stuff. The mess, the weirdness, the random bruises, and the awkward phone calls—this is what makes life (and sex) worth showing up for.

It's not about perfection. It's about laughing at yourself, loving the ridiculous, and knowing that even on the strangest days, you're still in the game.

And that's just Saturday.

Wait till you see what happens when the WiFi goes out, my neighbor's kid asks what a "cock ring" is, and I have to explain to my landlord why the smoke alarm keeps going off at 2 a.m. Truth is, I have no fucking idea. Won't happen again. Almost killed myself ripping the batteries out. I've heard dying by fire is one helluva bad way to go, but better than dealing with my landlord.

Unholy Communion

... the night that changed everything

*You don't realize how fake your
sex life was until someone
fucks you like they've got a
vendetta. — TechChick*

I never believed in "life-changing sex." Not the way they write about it
in magazines, not the way therapists promise it'll save your marriage,
not the way poets make it sound like a goddamn religious awakening.
Sex was fun, filthy, sometimes awkward, and always necessary. But
transformative? Please. That was a word for self-help books and
people who'd never had their face buried in a stranger's lap at 2 a.m.

Then there was that night.

It started with a dare. Not the cute kind. The kind that makes your skin prickle and your mouth go dry. He was new. New to me, new to the city, new to the kind of filth I'd been quietly collecting like rare coins. He had a voice that could melt glass and hands like loaded pistons ready to blow me apart.

We skipped the bar. Went straight to my place. No small talk. Just a look. That look. The one that says, I'm going to fuck you so hard you'll lose your goddamn mind.

Clothes hit the floor before the door even closed. My shirt caught on the doorknob, ripped, and I didn't care. He shoved me against the wall, mouth on my neck, teeth scraping, tongue hot and hungry. I could feel his cock, hard and heavy, pressing through his jeans. He didn't ask. He didn't need to.

He dropped to his knees. No warm-up, no negotiation. Just hands on my thighs, spreading me, mouth open, tongue flat and wet, dragging up my slit. He licked like he'd been waiting his whole life to taste me. I grabbed his hair, pulled him closer. He groaned... deep, guttural, vibrating against my clit. My knees buckled. He held me up with one arm, the other hand sliding up to pinch my nipple, rolling it between his fingers, tugging until I gasped for air.

He sucked my clit, slow at first, then harder, tongue flicking, lips sealed tight. I came so fast I almost punched him. He didn't stop. Just kept going, licking me through it, sucking every last tremor out of me. When I tried to pull away, He growled, bit my thigh, and went back in. I came so hard I was sure I'd blacked out. I caught my breath in ragged gasps before his next stroke found me again. I was shaking, legs jelly, heart pounding so loud I thought it would burst right out of my chest.

He stood up, wiped his mouth on the back of his hand, and kissed me. Hard. I could taste myself on his lips. He pushed me to my knees, unzipped, and let his cock slap against my tongue. Thick, salty, perfect. I sucked him slow, spit dripping down my chin, hands wrapped around his shaft, stroking, squeezing, twisting. He fucked my mouth, slow at first, then faster, hips rolling, hands tangled in my hair.

He pulled out, drug me to the bed. Threw me down, face-first, ass up. No words. Just a slap. Sharp, stinging, making me cry out. He slid two fingers inside me, curling and sweeping every ridge until my vision went white. He fucked me with his fingers, thumb on my clit, other hand gripping my hair, pulling my head back so he could whisper in my ear.

"You like being used, don't you?"

I moaned. Nodded. Couldn't speak. Didn't want to.

He lined up behind me, cock pressing at my entrance, slow... so slow I thought I'd scream. Then he slammed in, hard, deep, filling me, stretching me, making me forget every lover before him. He fucked me like he owned me. Like he was trying to fuck the memory of every other man out of my body.

He reached around, fingers on my clit, rubbing, circling, pinching. He bit my shoulder, left a mark. I came again, harder this time, screaming into the pillow, body convulsing, cunt gripping his cock so tight he grunted with effort.

He pulled out, flipped me over, pinned my wrists above my head. His mouth on my tits, biting, sucking, tongue flicking over my nipples. He slid down, tongue back on my clit, sucking, licking, two fingers inside me, curling, stroking. I came again until my body trembled beyond trembling. Tipping on the edge of oblivion, I gulped down air and steadied my racing heart as he paused, just long enough for me to remember where I was.

Then he crawled up, cock in hand, rubbed the head against my lips. I opened, took him deep, gagged, drooled, eyes watering. He fucked my mouth until he was close, pulled out, jerked himself, and came all over my tits, my neck, my face. Hot, sticky, filthy. I licked my lips, tasted him, smiled with satisfaction.

He collapsed next to me, both of us a mess of sweat, cum, spit, and bruises. He looked at me. Really looked. Not like I was a conquest. Like I was a fucking revelation.

I realized then: this wasn't just sex. This was surrender. This was worship. This was two people so hungry for each other they'd burn down the world just to taste a little more.

That night changed everything. I stopped pretending sex was just a game. I stopped faking, stopped performing, stopped holding back. I wanted it all. Raw, filthy, honest, real.

And I never settled for less again.

Welcome to the new religion. No apologies. No fake orgasms. No regrets. Nothing less will ever suffice.

Sex Laws According to Tech-Chick

... pretty sure I'm right

*Somewhere, a lawmaker is
banning anal while jerking
off in a Holiday Inn. America!*
— TechChick

Some days I feel like a goddamn genius. Other days I think my vibrator's outworking me. But on balance? Not bad. It's been a damn good ride and one that continues.

One thing is for certain: it's been a highly enlightening process. The overall experience as porn webmistress and sex advisor has taught me a few things that I would never have learned if not for all the funny, crazy, and endearing letters from my readers. To them goes my thanks and gratitude.

Getting mail from both men and women made me realize just how incredibly different we are. We couldn't be more different from each other if we were built from opposite molds, and actually, I think we were.

Women: suck more dick, talk less, love football, don't bitch.

Men: pick up your socks, stop sulking, say your feelings, hate porn.

In other words: we're all supposed to be someone else. Good luck with that.

The End. Piece of cake. Now, where's my zillion-dollar check?

Other stuff I've learned over the years:

- Masturbation is a very good thing for your sex life. You can't really do too much of it.

- Treating a man's dick like an object of worship will get a woman a long way in life.

- Be as uninhibited in your sex life as you possibly can. This always, always, always makes for the best sex.

- Keeping sex on the brain makes you want to fuck more, and the more you fuck, the more you wanna fuck.

- Don't stay with a partner who doesn't love sex. Life is too short.

- Slow and erotic is great, but don't knock the quick and dirty.

- People don't kiss enough. The best kissers are the best lays.

- The G-spot is a bunch of bullshit. I am quadrupling down on this one.

- People don't spend enough time on foreplay. Often, it's the best part of sex.

- People don't fuck enough, and doggy-style is way underrated.

- If you learn nothing else from this book, let it be this: Eat pussy like it's your last meal on earth.

That's it. That's the law (according to me, TechChick). Break it at your own risk.

True E-Tales from the Inbox

... no, you haven't heard it all

Every email starts with 'This is probably weird.' And then proves it. — TechChick

"TC, do you like to have sex?"
That's a real question I once got in my inbox.
To my adult website.

On a page labeled About Me.
I wish I could say it was the dumbest one I ever received, but no. That was just a typical Tuesday.

People email me everything. The sweet, the heartbroken, the sincerely confused. The ones who think I'm a priest, a pornographer, a therapist, a prostitute, or all four. Sometimes, all in the same sentence.

They ask if they're normal.
They ask how to last longer, how to feel something, how to ask for what they want without getting laughed out of the room.
They ask how to tell their wife they're bi.
Or their husband that they don't want to fake it anymore.
Or themselves that maybe they're not broken, they just never had a partner who gave a fuck.

And then there are the others. The ones who just want to "talk."
Or "meet up."
Or "grab coffee and see what happens."
They ask if I'm married.
They ask if I'm real.
They ask if I've ever had sex with a fan.
When I don't answer, they follow up.
"Okay, fine. At least tell me how to hook up with a pornstar."

Sure.

Step one: grow up.
Step two: bring cash.
Step three: be hot, rich, or extremely lucky.
Preferably all three.

But here's the thing no one expects when they write to me:

168

Underneath the cringe, the chaos, and the cumshot fantasies, there's something deeper.

People aren't just horny.
They're hungry.
For connection.
For answers.
For someone (anyone) to say,
"You're not a freak. You're just honest."

And yeah, some of them are unhinged.
Some are dangerous.
Some just need a nap and a hobby.
But some?
Some are beautiful. Messy and searching, and brave in ways they'll never admit out loud.
They don't want to shock me.
They want to be seen.
And if you're brave enough to hit send, you deserve an answer. Even if it's just a simple, "You're not alone."

So no.
You haven't heard it all.
But I have.
And if I've learned anything, it's this:
If you ask a real question—
The kind that hurts to type,
The kind that makes you nervous to hit send,
The kind you've been holding in for far too long—
I'll still read it.
And if I have something to say, I'll write you back.
Because someone should.
And apparently, that someone's me.

... A Day in the Life: Of E-Tales

Wake up. Check inbox. Regret checking inbox.

Scan a subject line that says "DO NOT DELETE THIS MESSAGE." Delete it.

Open one that starts, "Hi, I know this is weird, but I'm 19 and I think I'm addicted to..."
Of course you are.

Ignore twelve emails that want me to collab on some new, tweaked-out sex toy. (Jesus, this is my life now.)

Open one that just says, "TC... do you like... it?"
It.
That's the whole question.
I assume he means sex.
I hope he means sex. This one still bugs me to this day.

Open another from a guy who thinks a 'vulva' is a car. I really can't help that man.

Then another asks you if they can train their girlfriend to bark during sex.

Read a five-paragraph saga from a guy who wants to confess to cheating on his wife with her cousin. Twice. At Thanksgiving.
Delete. Reopen.
Decide I'm not qualified.

Take a break, do some yoga. Just kidding. I eat a Pop-Tart and wonder if I've become desensitized to shock. I already know the answer, but I sometimes fuck with myself.

But then...

There's one from a woman. Long. Raw. Brave.
She thanks me for helping her feel seen.
She says she left a toxic relationship.
She says she bought a vibrator and rediscovered her body.
She says she laughed. And cried.
And for a second, I forget all the cum, cats, and cousin-fuckers.

This is why I still open the mail.

That, and let's be honest, some of you are batshit, and I live for the story.

By 2pm, I'm drinking wine and deleting another apology email from a guy who opened with "U up?" and ended with "You're not like other women, I respect you."

I used to wonder if people were trolling.
Now, I just wonder if I'm the weird one. Because I keep answering.

Maybe I'm the voyeur now. Not of sex—but of honesty. The accidental confessions. The nervous laughter. The fucked-up beauty of it all.

I don't always know what to say. But I always listen.

And honestly? That might be the most honest thing I've said all day.

But if I stopped, who would read all your stories?

Another week begins. Mondays wish they were this weird.

Webmistress: The Dirty Truth

... oh fuck it, I'll tell (expanded confession)

> People think porn is the dirty
> part. It's not. The inbox is.
> — TechChick

I feel like my life is one shenanigan, followed by another, and another, and...

I lost my virginity at 16. His name was Barry. He was 26. (What a dick.) He wanted to take me for a ride in his red Corvette. Of course it was red. He gave me crabs. Of course he gave me crabs.

I've hooked up with someone just because they had really good air conditioning. I regret nothing.

I've used the "I'm on my period" excuse when I absolutely was not. I just didn't want to see his face anymore.

I've pretended to be asleep to avoid morning sex. Twice in the same week. He didn't buy it. I told him to fuck off and go die.

I've answered fan mail in my underwear, nipple clamp on my favorite nipple, eating cold pizza, judging people for their kinks.

I've said "I'm not usually like this" more times than I can count. I'm exactly like this.

I've fallen in love over a good kiss. I've faked love over good dick. I've ignored the gut feeling that said, "Get out," and stayed because I didn't want to be alone again.

I've had sex I didn't want, just to feel wanted. I've lied to someone I loved because I didn't know how to say "I need help."

I've been the other woman. I've also been the woman who got cheated on and thought it was her fault.

I've said "it's just sex" when it wasn't. I've cried in the shower so no one would hear me.

And sometimes, when I give advice, I wonder if I'm even qualified— or just really good at pretending I've figured it out.

So if you thought I was judging you? Trust me, my friend. I'm just as much of a mess.

And that's the dirty truth.

.

Final Thoughts

... final fuckery

We all want to be loved. Some
of us just start with licking.
— TechChick

So here we are. End of the line. Or the edge of the bed.

If you made it this far, you've officially read a sex book that didn't try
to save your soul or sell you a jade egg.

I didn't write this to make you better in bed.
I wrote it to remind you that being *human* in bed is enough.

The fumbling. The crying. The mismatched libidos.
The mystery stains. The porn tabs you forgot to close.
This is the real sex ed.

I hope to god you laughed at least once with your pants off.

If something I said helped you moan louder, leave faster, love smarter, or fake it less—hell yes.

And if you still have questions, good.
You're not broken. You're curious. Stay that way.

The world doesn't need more perfect lovers.
It needs more honest ones.

So go forth.
Fuck wisely.
Lick enthusiastically.
Ask the question.
Say the thing.
Wear the harness.
Burn the rules.

And when it gets messy—and it *will*—
don't shrink from it. Don't pretend. Don't delete the part that's most true.

I'll be over here.
Watching.
Writing.
Judging just a little.
And rooting for you the whole filthy way.

Dead? Bitch, Please.

... TechChick in 2025: 2.0 & counting

If you're reading this, you survived the shitstorm that was Sex Bytes 1.0. Congrats. You've got stamina.

What's changed since then? Some things. Not everything.
I ran a few sites.
I did nothing.
I ran more sites. I did even more nothing.
I answered even weirder emails. And yes, still judging you. Lovingly.

Now it's 2025. The world's a dumpster fire with better Wi-Fi.
I'm older. Filthier. Maybe wiser. *Maybe.*

TechChick.me is live:
More stories. More "Did she actually say that?" moments. And a weekly column I probably wrote in my underwear.

If you want in, stick around.
If you're easily offended... well, you made it this far. So maybe you're not.

Sex Bytes 2.0—the book—is coming soon. Why a sequel? Because the questions haven't stopped.
If anything, they've gotten louder. Weirder. And honestly, more important.

Sex is still confusing as hell.
And apparently, I'm still the one you want to ask.

Keep Exploring...

New columns every week:
Rants, sex Q&A, and filthy wisdom at **TechChick.me**

Want more Sex Bytes?
Get the **full audiobook** (perfect for listening to in bed with headphones of course), bonus content, and **exclusive discounts** on future Sex Bytes 2.0 drops at **GetSexBytes.com**

Yeah, I felt tacky putting links in here.
But my accountant said, "You're broke. At least TRY to pay your rent."

Thank Fuck for You

... you made this possible

Thanks for riding this out with me. Whether you've been here since the dial-up days or just stumbled in, you're the reason I keep doing this. The questions, the chaos, the confessions—they're all part of the story. And the story's not done.

To everyone who ever sent a wild question, an honest confession, or a "you changed my life" or "you ruined my relationship (but thanks anyway)" email—thank you.

To my accidental mentors, my ride-or-die crew, my dog who's seen too much shit, my now-dead cat, and even my accountant (who still can't believe this is a real job)—thank you.

To my accidental mentors, my ride-or-die crew, my dog who's seen too much shit, my now-dead cat, and even my accountant (who still can't believe this is a real job), thank you.

Here's to the next shitshow, the next question, and the next story we'll all pretend never happened.

Now go do something you'll regret. Then write me about it. My inbox is always open at **techchick.me.**

P.S. If you ever figure it all out, email me. I'll believe it when I see it.

XXXtras "They" Made Me Cut

... too filthy, too true, too late

WARNING: This is the stuff my editor, Janice (yes, Janice), threatened to quit over. If you're still reading, you're my people.

Okay. "They" is that "editor" I mentioned a couple of times. Yeah, she was cheap. If it's too good to be true... ah, fuck it.

183

So, during the "editing" process, I approved none of her suggestions. For example, she wouldn't shut up about me using too many em dashes—which is bullshit, by the way.

But what does Miss Smarty-Pants-Know-It-All TechChick do? Listens to her one time. This time. When she said, "Cut this entire section, or I quit!" (There we go with exclamation points again. So stressful.)

So here we are. I'm not even sure if she's alive anymore. I probably gave her an early heart attack.

I'm sticking this "No way!" section smack-dab here for your reading pleasure.

And if you're still alive, Janice?
Fuck the fuck off.

I once ghosted a guy mid-blowjob because he said, "You like that, huh? You want Daddy's yogurt?"
No, Brad. Nobody wants your yogurt. Not even your fucking probiotics.

I once sexted the wrong person. Twice. The second time was to a family member. We don't speak anymore.
Honestly, fair.

I've had sex on a grave. Not near a grave—on it. Headstone left a dent in my back. I'd do it again.
And no, you sickos—it wasn't Janice's grave.

I once pegged a guy while his wife watched from the kitchen, making risotto.
The risotto was excellent.

He wanted me to spit in his mouth and say, "You're just a hole." So I did. Twice.
He tipped well.

One guy begged me to edge him for three hours. I made it for 30 minutes, then ordered Thai food and let him cry.

Once had a guy ask if he could pay me to dress up as his stepmom and ruin his credit score.
I dressed up as his stepmom—then backed out when he handed me his Social. I'm filthy, not felonious.

I once agreed to a hookup with a guy I didn't like—just because he had blackout curtains, a clean shower, and working central air.
I'm not ashamed. I was hot, I was tired, I was moisturized.
10/10, would do it again.

I've watched cam girls fake orgasms so well I questioned my own for a week.

One guy once asked me to rate his dick. I told him, "It's a solid 6.5, but your personality is a soft 2."
He said, "That's harsh."
I said, "That's charity."

One guy once asked if I'd ever consider doing a live seminar called "How to Fuck Like You Write."
I told him I already do. It's called **this book**.

I've given advice while high. I've given advice while crying. I've given advice while actively regretting the last person I slept with.

And I've had moments, quiet ones, late at night, where I wondered if I'm just some sarcastic mirror people project their sex chaos onto.

Sometimes, I think I am.
Sometimes, I like it.

I've had women write in to thank me for helping them cum for the first time at age 34.
And men who ask if it's normal to cry after sex.
It is.
It really is.

There are days I feel like a therapist, a porn historian, a reluctant domme, and a human venting machine—usually all before noon.
Those are the days I drink at lunch.

People think sex advice is about technique.
It's not. **It's about permission.**
To want what you want.
To say what you need.
To stop pretending that sex is supposed to be clean, or flawless, or romantic, or performative, or anything besides yours.

So yeah, this chapter didn't make the original cut.
Too dirty.
Too chaotic.
Too real.
According to Janice, the "editor."

But if you're still here, reading this?

I love you. A. Lot.

www.ingramcontent.com/pod-product-compliance
Lightning Source LLC
Chambersburg PA
CBHW051422090426

42737CB00014B/2789